D1512318

"Matthew's story is a powerful example of how amazing life becomes when you follow the daily nudges of the Holy Spirit in your heart. His life experience of helping others will inspire you to step out of your comfort zone and live the adventure Jesus has for you!"

Joyce Meyer, Bible teacher, bestselling author

"Every believer would benefit from reading *One Small Step*. At times we all fall into complacency and live unaware of what God wants to do through us. Matthew Barnett teaches us how to be mindful of the promptings of God so that we can be available to take part in His work here on earth. The stories found within these chapters and the impactful biblical teachings make this resource a life-giving read for anyone wanting to wholeheartedly follow God."

Lysa TerKeurst, #1 *New York Times* bestselling author;
president, Proverbs 31 Ministries

"We all want to make a difference as we follow the example of Jesus, but we can easily feel overwhelmed by where to start. In *One Small Step*, Matthew Barnett shows us how to begin from where we are. When we follow the Holy Spirit's guidance and faithfully follow through on His prompting, we discover that we can be Jesus to others every day. With powerful insight from God's Word and memorable stories that will inspire you, *One Small Step* will lead you to take giant strides for God's Kingdom."

Chris Hodges, senior pastor, Church of the Highlands;
author, *The Daniel Dilemma* and *What's Next?*

"If I was to take advice from anyone about how to walk in faith, stay humble and accomplish great things for God, I would take it from Matthew Barnett. With the relentless commitment of an Energizer Bunny, Pastor Matthew has been serving the needy of Los Angeles with an intense and joyful commitment rarely seen in the City of Angels. In fact, the angels in this city pretty much all reside at the Dream Center, where those souls who have been labeled a lost cause are resurrected by the care of Matthew, his wife, Caroline, and all the wonderful people who have committed to helping 'the least of these.'"

Patricia Heaton, award-winning actress and author

ONE SMALL STEP

ONE SMALL STEP

THE LIFE-CHANGING
ADVENTURE OF FOLLOWING
GOD'S NUDGES

MATTHEW
BARNETT

Chosen
a division of Baker Publishing Group
Minneapolis, Minnesota

Published by Chosen Books
11400 Hampshire Avenue South
Bloomington, Minnesota 55438
www.chosenbooks.com

Chosen Books is a division of
Baker Publishing Group, Grand Rapids, Michigan

Printed in the United States of America

ISBN 978-0-8007-9957-1

Library of Congress Cataloging-in-Publication Control Number: 2019051197

This book is dedicated to my wonderful wife, Caroline, and my two precious children, Caden and Mia, for the way they have embraced the messy aspects of ministry (while loving every second of this outrageous calling and roller-coaster journey).

CONTENTS

Foreword by Jentezen Franklin   11

Acknowledgments   13

Introduction   15

STEP 1   Follow the Nudge   19

STEP 2   A Life-Changing Step   33

STEP 3   The Steps You Think You Cannot Take   49

STEP 4   Make Everything a Big Deal   61

STEP 5   The Small Steps That Change Lives   73

STEP 6   Step on Toes   87

STEP 7   Step Out of Yourself   101

STEP 8   When You Feel You Cannot Move   119

STEP 9   One Small Thought   133

STEP 10   The Attitude of a Servant   149

STEP 11   The Risk-Taking Step   165

STEP 12   Step to the Future   185

STEP 13   Leave a Local Legacy   203

FOREWORD

In *One Small Step: The Life-Changing Adventure of Following God's Nudges*, Matthew Barnett spells out God's plans for our changing the world—and those society has left behind. Small step after small step is the path I have watched Matthew walk through the years, covering an incredible amount of territory. No one has stayed the course and covered more ground, step by step, nudge after nudge, than Matthew and his amazing team at the Dream Center. Life after life, one day at a time, meeting every crisis with the love of Jesus and compassion that is unparalleled, the Los Angeles Dream Center is a refuge from a thousand storms.

In this groundbreaking book, Matthew provides the formula for stepping off the boat for any brave soul who would dare to do the same. It's a must-read for any young pastor searching for a way to make a difference in the lives of the most marginalized in our modern society. And for every seasoned pastor looking for the next move of God in your church, this could very well be the call He is asking you and your congregation to answer.

This is not a book for the faint of heart or for those wanting to punch that nine-to-five time clock. Human need doesn't keep bankers' hours, and the immediate needs of a desperate soul may wake you in the middle of the night. But if you dare to take a glimpse at life on the front lines of the battle for the souls of the forgotten, then this book is for you.

It has been our honor to partner with the Dream Center over the years and to watch them answer the call to help the homeless, those caught up in sex trafficking or veterans at the end of themselves ready to take their lives. Every time Matthew says yes, the miracles start to happen. Not big and loud miracles. No, the kind of miracles that never make the papers—such as an addict celebrating thirty days of sobriety or the homeless man who receives his first paycheck or moves into his first apartment. Miracles like these happen every day, but not without those small steps of preparation and organization that it takes to pull it off. These are the nuts and bolts that build the launching pads of a thousand lives—and thousands more . . . little by little, day after day, in a city that never sleeps. It's all here to see as Matthew lays out the blueprint for any who dare to reproduce this kind of love in *your* city that never sleeps.

Lastly, to whom much is given, much is required, and that's a weighty responsibility. Matthew hasn't been able to do this all by himself, and neither will you. But know this: For each and every person who dares to walk this path, the Lord has already started moving on the hearts of those who will someday help you in ways you never could have imagined. Allow Matthew to tell you some of these kinds of stories in the pages ahead. Allow each chapter to move you to action as the Lord begins to surround you with the army He is raising up to go with you. It's all here on the pages ahead. And I know of no better tour guide than Matthew Barnett. He knows where every land mine has been planted and where every ambush has been set. He has experienced victory after victory and has the scars to tell their stories.

Jentezen Franklin, senior pastor, Free Chapel

ACKNOWLEDGMENTS

With joy and gratitude, I acknowledge the members of the Dream Center family who continue to walk on water while keeping their eyes on Jesus, extending a life jacket to others at the same time.

Many thanks to our amazing friends at Chosen Books, who champion a message of service and surrender, for encouraging me to write this book, and to my father, Tommy Barnett, who inspired so much of this book with the way he models adventure and who has never lost sight of the fact that ministry is all about the "one."

Special thanks to my mother, Marja, who taught me that you can have fun and still be a Christian, as well as my brother, Luke, and sister, Kristie, who would fight a bear to protect their baby brother.

Finally, I also want to acknowledge everyone living at the Dream Center who is dreaming from rock bottom—you amaze me with your courage to rise from the ashes and embrace God's "next."

INTRODUCTION

The bedtime Bible stories we tell our children are truly wonderful. David taking a few smooth stones, placing them in a slingshot and launching them toward the forehead of a giant, knocking him out. The Red Sea being rolled back so people could walk on dry ground. Daniel surviving a hungry den of lions. We put our children to bed, telling them stories of people who chose to *step out*. Then as they get older, we teach them how to avoid risk, play it safe and make a comfortable living. It is the ultimate contrast to God's Word: Jesus, ignoring criticism and going out of His way to talk to a broken woman by the well, or in the last minute reaching out to a criminal next to Him on the cross, giving him eternal life. The entire life of Jesus involved stepping out into the unknown and bringing life to a broken world. Yet more typically we run from the people we fear.

The church I pastor is called the Dream Center. Think of a big four-hundred-thousand-square-foot hospital that sits like a ship next to the Hollywood freeway, open every day for anyone with a need. People who have addictions, homeless families, veterans, kids who age out of the foster care system who need a place to live and victims of human trafficking—all find shelter in our building, free of charge. It is the ultimate Motel 6 that will leave the light on for you. The reason we call it the Dream Center is because we believe that vision, courage and life purpose is the greatest way to come alive. We do not believe people are junkies or addicts, but rather people with misplaced passion.

No roller coaster ride at Six Flags could ever compare with the decades of ups and downs of working with these most broken, vulnerable and shattered lives. There once was a time when I would come to my office and maybe two or three people would walk into our facility throughout the day to get help. Sad to say, those days are over. Los Angeles is almost unrecognizable, because homelessness is so widespread. The new norm is people lining up out the door wanting to get into our recovery program, hoping for one last chance to change; a mother and child riding on the last tank of gas sputter into our parking lot, hoping for a place to stay and rebuild.

It is this endless assault of everyday need that will provide a background to this book. Do I have all the answers? No! Not even close. This book is not about solutions; in fact, it is about something greater. It is about doing good and having no clue how to make sense of it. It is about the Holy Spirit, the encounters we face daily and the willingness to break free from a me-centered world to embrace the messy life of someone who is willing to step out. It is about taking risks for people who most others would say deserve their fate, dreaming for people who have lost their dreams and refusing to give in to reasons that hold back compassion.

The Dream Center hides under the shadow of the famous Hollywood sign as a contrast to culture. We think of it as a place that picks up the broken pieces of those who fail to find the Hollywood Dream. We are the last stop for those who have nowhere else to go. Not that we are perfect. Most of the time, nothing makes sense, and we make mistakes all the time. We constantly live on the edge, taking in more people than we can pay for. We do not have the magic formula for solving society's problems, and we have not cornered the market on compassion. We are simply people who believe that stepping out is a better option than playing it safe.

A well-intentioned man asked me this question at a pastor's conference: "Pastor Matthew, if I started a work like the Dream Center, what could go wrong?" I looked at him and said, "Everything can. In fact, everything *will* go wrong!" He looked sad after my response, and I knew right away that, in his mind, the risk of opening a place like this was just too high. I could tell by his concern for danger and the unknown that he would probably not do what his heart was telling him to do. It is not easy to step out, but it is rewarding, even life-changing.

People are unpredictable, and helping your neighbors is a messy business, a counterintuitive thing to do in our safe, predictable, American culture. When you decide to step out, you will be labeled irresponsible and reckless, and your motives will be questioned. Even so, I would still suggest that every day you follow the nudge of the Holy Spirit. Step out and do what He is asking you to do.

This is not a book about random acts of kindness, but rather a book about Holy Spirit encounters—encounters that nudge us toward making a difference in the world around us. As a kid I used to read books that were part of a series called Choose Your Own Adventure. You would read a part of the book, and it would tell you to turn to another page. You would read that portion of the book, and you would be offered options as to which storyline you would like to follow. In other words you, the reader, could decide which path you wanted the story to take.

That is similar to the decisions we face every day. Let's decide to go on a wonderful adventure of serving humanity! Let's follow God's adventure for our lives.

STEP 1

Follow the Nudge

Since I was a child growing up in church, I have heard the phrase "the dead coming back to life." I will admit that the line has always creeped me out. Avid Christ followers would say it at Sunday school or in casual conversations and I always found it to be strange. All my young brain could think of was Michael Jackson's "Thriller" music video, with zombies limping along the highway to a killer music beat. I am sure that the reason it always struck me as strange is that it is such an extreme statement. I do believe God does miracles, and I know that anything is possible, but the dead coming back to life? Now, that is extreme.

One day early in the morning, around 6:00 a.m., a woman I will call Valeria was roaming the parking lot of the Dream Center. I pulled up to my parking space and saw this young woman, who was clearly possessed by something. She was high on meth and completely disoriented. Her sweet, desperate mom did not know what to do, so she had dropped her off at the Dream Center before work. This is a regular event at our place. We are known to be a place of last resort to so many. Many times, parents will tell their sons or daughters that our recovery program is a thirty-day rehab just to get them through the door. They know it is a year long, but they are so desperate to get them off the streets that they will do whatever they can to get them into a safe place.

The first thing that came to my mind when I saw Valeria was, *How can I sneak past her and not make eye contact?* Isn't that an awful thing for me to think? Matthew Barnett, the pastor of the Dream Center, the champion of the forgotten, did not want to go out of his way to help a struggling woman on meth. Selfishly, I looked for a way around this tortured soul. Even after 25 years of ministry (I want to be transparent right out of the gate), there are times when I love my routine more than I love people. I, the so-called expert on helping hurting people, find myself to be far more self-centered than I want to be.

This story would be much better if I could say that I went out of my way to go up to her and ask the question, "How can I serve you?" But the truth is, she tracked me down. Looking into her eyes, I could see she had the countenance of a dead woman walking. The only request of this tired soul was, "Can you help me?" I collected myself and said, "Sure, if you go up the elevator with me, I will take you to our women's one-year recovery program." She agreed. Reluctantly and out of total obligation, I took her up in our old hospital elevator to the eleventh floor that our women call home.

The elevator door slowly opened, and facing this young woman was a check-in desk. She was afraid. Paranoia set in as the drugs played tricks on her mind. She thought we were going to take her in, kidnap her, cause her harm. Immediately, she wanted to go back down. Drugs can truly distort your mind when it comes to trust. Then, something amazing happened. The best way I can describe it is with the lyrics of the famous song "Love Lifted Me," written by James Rowe in 1912:

I was sinking deep in sin, far from the peaceful shore,
Very deeply stained within, sinking to rise no more.
But the Master of the sea heard my despairing cry,
From the waters lifted me, now safe am I.

Love lifted me! Love lifted me!
When nothing else could help, love lifted me.
Love lifted me! Love lifted me!
When nothing else could help, love lifted me!

The women who were in the program did not have the same attitude I had in the parking lot. They did not see this event unfolding as a "*Have* to serve" moment; they saw it as a "*Get* to serve moment." They rushed to this woman as if to say, "We want one more woman in our family!" They surrounded her and put their arms around her. Suddenly *love* became the strongest drug in the building. Love reached through the chemical-induced trauma and settled Valeria down. In a split second, these women had made the decision to come to the rescue. I learned in that moment that miracles happen because of sudden, quick decisions made by people who run to rescue the tormented.

We can miss our moment to make a difference by rationalizing the encounter away. It is amazing how much a seasoned pastor can learn from courageous women a few months into a recovery program. The most broken human beings can often show the experienced believer what love looks like. That kind of love is raw, real and not mechanical. The kind of love that does not have

> The most broken human beings can often show the experienced believer what love looks like.

time to consider if compassion should be granted. It just pounces on the afflicted with pure grace, without overthinking the worthiness of the recipient.

Love certainly lifted Valeria. A year later, I saw her on the stage at church with her graduation diploma, smiling at the crowd that was wildly cheering for her. I saw it! A dead person had come back to life. Now I know what those old-timers in the church had been saying to me for years. It is never too late for a resurrection and nothing is impossible with God. The dead can come back to life through the power of love. Split-second decisions, responding to people's needs, following the nudge of compassion—that is what serving God is all about.

One Act of Compassion at a Time

This book is not for the safe at heart; it is for those who want to live dangerously, outside of the normal flow of a me-centered world. This book is not for people who point to the government or the pastor down the street as the solution. Ordinary people make a difference in everyday life, turning a nation around, one act of compassion at a time. It is not always easy to love like that. Major change feels hard. Problems in life can feel so overwhelming that people give up, thinking, *Why even try?*

The city I call home, Los Angeles, is facing a homeless epidemic unlike anything we have ever seen before. The latest count by the Los Angeles Homeless Service Authority found that there are over sixty thousand homeless people in Los Angeles. One night I was driving home from a Los Angeles Lakers game, and I saw the cardboard boxes used as homes for the homeless lining the on-ramp to the freeway. The boxes were so shockingly close to the road that if a car turned too wide or a driver had imbibed one too many drinks, they could easily slam into the homeless encampment. It was enough to make me pull up to the driveway of my home and begin to weep, saying, "Why even try? The problems are too big, society is so broken, I think I'll just quit." It is easier to live life that way, to lose heart, to decide to protect your own stuff. After all, everything can so easily be taken away.

Really, it is not just about helping homeless people, it is about helping everyone. Some of the poorest people I know live in some of the wealthiest zip codes. I once asked a wealthy man what was the one thing he loved the most about his life. His answer was, "Going home to my expensive liquor cabinet."

People are in need, but so many times we feel restrained and held back in our efforts to offer a helping hand. We may feel a nudge about a need, but then excuses pile up and our insecurity and fear hold us back. I know this for certain because, even after many years of loving the unlovable, the battle rages on inside me. One side of me wants to serve others and the other side is loaded with excuses for why I cannot move in that direction. When it comes to compassion, sometimes it feels like I am in a bad dream. I want to move, but my feet feel stuck in quicksand, unable to do what my heart wants.

> When it comes to compassion, sometimes it feels like I am in a bad dream. I want to move, but my feet feel stuck in quicksand, unable to do what my heart wants.

For 25 years, I have served the homeless and have had the honor of helping thousands of people transfer from having nothing to having a future. A life of serving others is all that I've known since I was given my first opportunity to pastor at twenty years of age. With God, we have built an extraordinary place called the Dream Center, where notorious gang members find freedom and to which judges refer people rather than to prison.

However, when I lose heart, I must fight against that layer of contentment that wants to keep down my best side, the serving side. I know that serving and responding to the nudges of the Holy Spirit will make me happy, yet I choose a life of selfishness—and sadness. Helping people will always create the ultimate high; it is the best drug. Yet I keep self-medicating by satisfying my own wants and desires, resisting the better voice of the Holy Spirit that calls me to love. The best side of me is right there, but rebellion causes me to build a soundproof room in my heart where I cannot sense the nudge of God's call to serve.

Others do not see this side of me. Instead, they see the side that has to put on a good face to keep people encouraged. They do not see the wrestling match of my soul, the battle for control between the giver and the taker.

What does the best side look like? It is the side that is willing to follow the nudge of God. In today's culture we might call it "random acts of kindness," the idea of doing kind things for people out of the blue. Stepping out and helping people on a whim is a wonderful thing, but there's something deeper. The calling to do good is a lifelong orientation that does not take a day off and is not activated only during Christmastime and holidays. God wants us to understand the mandate of our calling, the fundamental value of living from a permanent stance of service. He wants us to understand the idea of following the nudges of the Holy Spirit, doing things simply because God put a desire in our heart to do them. Someone who lives this lifestyle chooses to be led by the Spirit of God and is willing to obey. This person operates out of a heart of generosity; he or she is like a little Dream Center in a human body, operating counter to the culture of greed and self-gratification. This person prays intentional prayers that ask God to bring on divine encounters and for courage not to run from the need.

In Valeria's situation, those few steps that the women in the recovery program took completely changed her life. A warm embrace and a kind welcome were all she needed to turn the corner.

The Spirit of God will lead you every day to a spectacular life full of incredible experiences. If you truly open your heart and look around, you will see the opportunity for being a missionary in your own field every single day. We are not human beings struggling for survival, we are walking miracles following the nudges of the Holy Spirit, instigating change.

Little Acts of Kindness Rule the World

Whenever someone accomplishes something great and they reflect on their achievements, it always goes back to someone who took one small step to help them back at the very start. I find this incredible. It will always go back to a coach, a carpool mom, a wise waiter, a person who paid for someone's meal. It all adds up; it all matters. The big events of the world get all the headlines, but little acts of kindness rule the world.

When I started to pastor, no one wanted a twenty-year-old preacher. Then God sent me an angel in the form of an older man in his eighties named Gus. Gus followed the nudge of the Holy Spirit and told the church to get behind this young preacher. He saw something good in me. After the church started to gain momentum, I asked him why he had supported someone so inexperienced. His answer: "Because the Holy Spirit told me to be the one person who would believe in you unconditionally."

What would have happened if he had not responded to that nudge? What if he had restrained himself from saying what was in his heart to say? The truth is, I would have quit. He saved my life.

People all over the world are serving others in need. They are changing the world and do not even know it. Little acts of kindness matter and always have an impact beyond what we can recognize. People who serve in small ways are heavenly legends—famous in heaven yet underappreciated on earth.

Jesus is the best example of someone following the nudge. When He was tempted in the wilderness, He showed the price He was willing to pay for humankind. I am so glad Jesus responded to the nudge to go off into the wilderness; His simple act of going carries so much weight: "At once the Spirit sent him out into the wilderness, and he was in the wilderness forty days, being tempted by Satan. He was with the wild animals, and angels attended him" (Mark 1:12–13).

> Little acts of kindness matter and always have an impact beyond what we can recognize. People who serve in small ways are heavenly legends—famous in heaven yet underappreciated on earth.

Jesus wants us to know that He was tempted in the same way that we are, but He overcame it to become the Savior that we needed—a Savior able to defeat what defeats us. Jesus would hear things others would not hear, see things others would not see and be moved by things that others would not even pay attention to. He saw every detail of a person's need. In the same way, the closer we get to God, the more attentive we will become to the specific details of human need.

Over and over in the Scriptures, we see how Jesus went out of His way to minister to someone. He did not let His routines hold Him back. The pattern emerges continually; for Jesus, the immediate need of a man or a woman represented God's call for Him that day.

I feel that one of the hardest Scripture verses to live by is Proverbs 3:27, which says, "Do not withhold good from those to whom it is due, when it is in your power to act." What do I do? I find myself questioning pure things in my heart all the time. Fear crushes kindness before it even has the chance to make lift-off.

The spirit of fear opposes a Christian willing to break free from routine to make a difference. Fear constantly preys on faith to try to rip the spiritual legs out from under someone who has the audacity to believe that change is possible. The spirit of fear hates the boldness of trying to meet the needs of others. Fear will try to crush an idea before it ever takes form. It presents many questions but has no solutions. What if I help someone and it does not go right? What if they refuse my help? Even something as simple as helping someone with an extra dime at a gas station can feel like too much. You know it is the right thing to do, and you know you have the power to do it, but fear holds you back.

For my part, I have learned that the very fear of doing good is like a confirmation to overcome it, so that I can respond to the need that is right before me.

Just Do It

When we feel inspired to do something that we can do, why not just do it? Why not simply follow the nudges of the Holy Spirit and get used to feeling uncomfortable about the small things that the Holy Spirit calls us to do? God's promptings are occurring all day long. In order to make a difference in the world, we need to pray that we would open up our hearts. We need to give in to each nudge of the Holy Spirit.

Every school day I pick my kids up from school. About an hour before pick-up time, I start to think of ways I can bless my kids when I see them. Years ago, I felt the Holy Spirit telling me to make my car a place of refuge for my kids when they leave the classroom. I think it is important to get in the habit of doing little things with a lot of love.

> God's promptings are occurring all day long. In order to make a difference in the world, we would open up our hearts and give in to each nudge of the Holy Spirit.

I know how it feels. In my own life, at the end of the day in high school, I would come to the car so tired, even feeling a bit bullied by other students. My mom would always pull up early in the school line to get me. She would always be on time. Once I asked her why she was always so punctual and her response was so sweet. She said, "The earlier I pick you up, the more I get to see you." Every day she had a surprise for me. Some days she would just tell me how much she loved me; other days, she would take me to the store to buy a new music tape that had come out. (Yes, I am that old.) I could not wait to see my mom's car pull up at Thunderbird High School in Phoenix, Arizona. With each strike of the clock at school, I knew I was an hour closer to being in the care of my mother, who made the car a little place of escape. I used to play it off as if I were unimpressed, but my life was shaped by those moments. Those fifteen minutes in the car with Mom every day were some of the happiest moments of my childhood.

Now I find myself doing the same thing. Compassion increases from one generation to the next. I will get a Starbucks coffee for the kids or make them a playlist of songs to listen to on the way home. Or I will get them their favorite treat: acai bowls. I have tried hard not to ask the same questions that most parents ask, "How was your day?" or "How much homework do you have?" Instead, I just want to make their day a little brighter. My listening to that simple prompting has allowed my kids to experience a little oasis at the end of their school day, even if it is in a Dodge Caravan. I think it is amazing how little acts of kindness can become instinctive as we carry on the tradition of service to the next generation.

Anointed to Do Good

Do not rationalize away the voice of God when He whispers to you, even when He tells you to do insignificant things. Little things matter.

The nudges of the Holy Spirit are prompting us all the time, provoking us to do good and to breathe life into the circumstances around us. Just *follow the nudge*. Respond and take one small step toward doing good. Soon it becomes an exciting way to live your whole life. Soon you will find that rather than trying to simply survive the day, you can create an exciting day, living from moment to moment and taking the initiative rather than defending your own turf. The little things you decide to do for people create an appetite to do more for others.

Get used to following the nudge. The nudge most always will be in opposition to what your flesh wants, but the joy lies in ignoring what your flesh wants and surrendering to life outside of the safety net of ordinary living. Respond to what your *heart* says but your *mind* tries to hold back. Give—even when fear grips your heart. When even a whisper of a kind deed occurs to you, realize there is probably a one hundred percent chance it is God. It is His nature to do good all the time, and He wants to use you. James 1:17 says, "Every good and perfect gift is from above, coming down from the Father of the heavenly lights, who does not change like shifting shadows."

A one-sentence description of Jesus' life is found in Acts 10:38: "How God anointed Jesus of Nazareth with the Holy Spirit and power, and how he went around doing good and healing all who were under the power of the devil, because God was with him." He was anointed to do good and so are you. Open the door to your heart and listen to the promptings of the Holy Spirit. When you see an opportunity to do good, go for it. *Follow the nudge.* Depart from the shadows and start moving toward the bright side of life. Open your eyes and look around; see the extraordinary ways you can stop rationalizing yourself out of doing acts of kindness. Start saying yes to the things that bring life.

My daughter and I were walking into a restaurant and there was a homeless man asking for money. We walked past him and then my daughter said, "Dad, wait!"

I said, "Don't give this guy money. He might use it for drugs." She ran back to the man and gave him money anyway.

"Dad, I did it because God spoke to me, too." It was such a simple expression of faith, and so pure. We do not know what people will do with our kindness or if they will even take advantage of it, but that is not what is supposed to help us decide. It is only up to us to start paying attention to the nudge of the Spirit.

All around us we hear rules and guidelines that spell out what people should do. That is part of human culture. The nudges of the Holy Spirit are almost always countercultural. My prayer is that this book will lead us to err on the side of being people of response rather than people of excuses and limitations. Learn to trust the Spirit-led side of you that asks you to do things that are outside your familiar safe zone. You cannot live an extraordinary life by choosing to live in a place of containment. Do more things just because you feel the nudge of the Holy Spirit telling you to do them.

Have you ever seen a caged bird set free? How wonderful to see it fly out of containment and begin to soar! If you choose to follow the nudges of the Holy Spirit and take unusual chances, letting your life be a gift to the world, something beautiful gets released within your spirit. You will never regret learning to follow the nudge.

MY SMALL STEP 1

After reading about this step and taking some time to pray, write down the small step you will take to follow God's nudge.

STEP 2

A Life-Changing Step

I can remember the day so vividly. The entire staff was gathered together in the old chapel on the seventh floor of our hospital. It was an emergency meeting. Please forgive me for sounding so dramatic, but it was the worst day of my life as a pastor. We all experience a handful of times that take our breath away, days when the stress is so high it feels like we are living at an altitude too high to find air. This was not a meeting to announce good news; it was a meeting to announce the news that the Dream Center was going through the worst financial crisis in two decades. We had finished remodeling every floor of our hospital building by the year 2014 and had added nearly two hundred beds—an awful lot of extra people to house, feed and shelter. Honestly, in our eagerness to help as many people as possible, we probably grew too fast. That left us with a huge problem by 2016. We were in such a bind that we could not meet the payroll for the month.

How in the world could I face my staff to give them this news? We live in Los Angeles, where even working people can face homelessness by just missing a paycheck for two weeks. Fifteen minutes before the meeting, I was in my office trying to figure a way out.

Two things crossed my mind. First, I could call it quits, justifying to myself that a lot of good had been done over the past twenty years of ministry. Then I could ride off into the sunset, telling myself that it was a good run, but that all good things must come to an end. Or, second, I could take a step of faith that requires the kind of courage that makes you tremble, the kind of faith that hurts.

> I could ride off into the sunset, telling myself that it was a good run, but that all good things must come to an end. Or I could take a step of faith that requires the kind of courage that makes you tremble, the kind of faith that hurts.

I grew up in the home of Pastor Tommy Barnett, who would literally cut the word *cannot* out of the dictionary. So throwing in the towel was not a core conviction of my family heritage. I placed a call to the woman at the bank who handles my retirement fund, and I cashed out everything possible to help make the payroll for the next month to keep the Dream Center engine going. The woman asked me, "Are you sure you want to do this?" You know it is a big step of faith when your financial advisors think you have lost your mind.

When you have been called to do something great for God, you do not have the luxury of jumping out with a golden parachute like the CEO of a failing corporation. You must be willing to take life-changing steps without understanding how to survive it. You will feel all alone, you will feel irresponsible and you will feel out of balance. You have not yet truly lived until you are called upon to make a sacrifice that will test your faith and reveal if "Trust in God" is just a cute phrase or your true belief. Peter walked on water and then he sank. I think his sinking was just as much evidence of his faith as the walking, because true faith entails both walking and sinking.

On that, the hardest day of my life, I stood up in front of my staff to let them know that I had emptied the bank to keep the ship floating. I had to admit failure. No one wants to do that, and no one likes to feel that he has let someone down. It is especially difficult when it involves money.

When you give up all of your wealth and donate it back to the work of God, two things can happen. First, there is the struggle to give, because *things* play such a big role in our lives. We like our stuff. We also question our maturity or even our mental and emotional stability if we do something drastic at a moment's notice. At the same time, when you give something sacrificially, it sets you free in your soul. When you give until it hurts, it does something in you that reminds you that things do not have that much power over you. A certain kind of freedom sets in when devotion to the cause overtakes the need for security. Money can destroy families (and organizations), tear them apart and create wounds that will never heal. But when you let go of everything and you have nothing left, somehow you feel more alive than ever. It is like going on a scary roller coaster for the first time. Standing in line is the worst part, but once you get on board the ride, it is quite exciting. Radical devotion to God can give you a pretty awesome adrenaline rush!

The last thing we want to do when bad things come our way is to make a move. Usually, our first choice is to find a corner somewhere and just wait for the storm to pass over. Choosing faith when you are gripped by fear is a life-changing step. Maybe you are reading this book in the midst of the biggest battle of your life and you want to quit. I am saying to you: "Don't do it!" I know it is tempting (even alluring) to just quit. I know the truth of this Scripture from hard personal experience: "Let us not become weary in doing good, for at the proper time we will reap a harvest if we do not give up" (Galatians 6:9). In other words, keep taking small steps and keep your feet moving, even in the middle of fierce storms. Keep forward motion alive, whether it is one small step or a giant leap.

> Keep taking small steps and keep your feet moving, even in the middle of fierce storms. Keep forward motion alive, whether it is one small step or a giant leap.

World Marathon Challenge

The Dream Center survived that storm. God's Word and His promises always outlast a trial. It was as though the windows of heaven opened in response to making that bold move.

The biggest way out of our long-term financial struggle came in a very unusual way. One day I received a text from a friend telling me about this thing called the World Marathon Challenge. He sent me an article about these crazy people running seven marathons on seven continents on seven consecutive days. Please read that again to understand the magnitude of that statement. My friend said, "Pastor, I know you've run a marathon before. You can do this! It could be a great fundraiser to keep the Dream Center going!"

I wanted to reply to him the way Jesus replied to Peter, "Get thee behind me, Satan!" Have you ever met a person who is always volunteering you to do things he would not do himself? This was that guy. (His favorite Scripture was, "*You* can do all things through Christ who strengthens you.")

No, this did not feel like God talking. He went on to tell me how people could sponsor me to run the seven marathons on seven continents on seven consecutive days. I repeated that one more time for emphasis. You must understand the pure lunacy of this idea. My personal financial contribution got us out of temporary trouble, but what was my long-term strategy to help us go forward? I had no further strategy except this crazy idea that had now been presented to me.

A man from my church named Phil Liberatore called me and said, "Pastor, if you undertake this challenge, I will make the first gift of $100,000." Suddenly, I was more enticed by the idea. The deal was that when I said yes, he would write the check. So I agreed. Sometimes you just say yes and figure it out later. No way I could leave that much money on the table that could go to help so many people. Blindly I stepped out in an outrageous direction. I signed up to join an army of elite runners who run and train all the time. I was an amateur, a weekend running warrior, who had no business saying yes to something like this. The only reason I would run a few miles a day was so that I could eat donuts and balance out my daily caloric intake. The other people signing up for the World Marathon Challenge are the kind of husbands and wives who do marathon trips to celebrate wedding anniversaries. What normal people do that?

We started the fundraising campaign to raise support for the Dream Center. The campaign was called "Face Yourself," with the idea being that everyone has one great challenge in life that he or she needs to face and to take on. The marathons were symbolic of every person's specific battle. The challenge I had to face was overcoming my fear of blood clots returning. In 2013, I almost died of blood clots after playing in a church softball tournament. I had started having a tough time breathing after the

> Sometimes you just say yes and figure it out later.

37

tournament, and when I went to the doctor, it turned out I had pulmonary embolisms blocking both of my lungs. God had allowed me to escape the jaws of death by playing all day with clots blocking both lungs. This fear was very real to me as I considered the marathon. Running, riding on airplanes and fluid build-up in legs is not a good idea for someone with a high blood-clotting factor.

I trained and worked myself up to ninety miles a week. Calf pain, IT band pain, hamstring pain—I had to work through all of it just to build up enough base miles to take this on. That small step of saying yes was turning out to be a lot more than I had anticipated. Still, one small step of saying yes can lead to an incredible adventure. Initially, it had seemed so harmless to say yes to the challenge, but all of the preparatory work was unimaginable.

> One small step of saying yes can lead to an incredible adventure.

The day before I left to go on the World Marathon Challenge, I had an amazing send-off from the residents who live on campus at the Dream Center. I walked down the long hallway by my office to the elevator. This was the same walk I had taken nearly a year before to tell the staff we did not have money to keep going. However, this walk felt different; it was a walk of victory. The residents lined up all over the parking lot of the Dream Center, cheering me on, holding up signs and giving me high fives before I took off for the airport. Former drug addicts, mothers who were once homeless, veterans from our shelter—all of them cheering. I can still hear their cheers and see the image of that send-off in my mind, and I would never want to erase or delete it. Their gesture of encouragement became more fuel to my soul than I could have dreamed. And in reality, this run was about to dramatically change my life.

Seven Marathons, Seven Continents, Seven Days

The World Marathon Challenge took me first to Chile, where we set up base camp for a few days to talk about the adventure we were about to embark on. Thirty-three of us from all over the world were in the hotel conference room getting the rundown about this adventure. A former war veteran who had lost his arm in war was making the trip, as well as a blind woman named Sinead from Ireland. It was stunning to see such courageous people. The people in that room were not just alive—they were truly living.

Some of the best runners in the world, such as Mike Wardian, an ultradistance champion, walked into the briefing room. I was a bit starstruck by this modern-day mileage grinder (think Forrest Gump running all the way around the world). Everyone else there had some major running experience, and they also had big hearts for adventure along with running for great causes. I was by far the least experienced runner. (Well, you've got to be famous for something, right?)

We bonded for a day in Chile, got briefed on the adventure, and then we took a Russian cargo-type plane to Antarctica. When they told me about the seven continents, I forgot that Antarctica is a continent, or I never would have done this. (Thus, the reason it is important to pay attention in school during geography class. Otherwise, you will find yourself running a marathon on a glacier in below-freezing conditions.) The old plane was like something out of a Terminator movie, with wires hanging down from the ceiling and old seats; it looked like it had survived a war. I would not have been surprised to see someone with duct tape out on the wing trying to fix it.

We were told to put on these big, oversized red coats because when we landed, it was going to be unbearably cold. Also, we were instructed to wear sunglasses because the sun was so bright and its reflection off the ice could burn your eyeballs. (That's always a nice thing to hear upon arrival.) We unpacked and piled into an old Jeep and went four-wheeling on a glacier—probably the coolest thing I have ever experienced. Off-road trucking on ice? Now that is *living*!

People ask me what it was like in Antarctica. I felt that I was on another planet. I kept forgetting we were still on planet earth. The sun was so bright and the winds would shift whenever they decided they wanted to. The mountains were breathtaking, with perfect blue crystalline images shining from them. No, I did not see penguins, which was kind of a bummer.

We stayed in tents, and I had the tremendous joy of sharing mine with one of the greatest runners of all time: Ryan Hall, record-holding American in the Boston Marathon. He came out of retirement without even training just to raise awareness for the Dream Center. Throughout this adventure, he maintained such an even temperament and positive attitude. It reminded me why some people are the best at what they do. Ryan had a peace with God that was so real he could curtail the panic of any stressful moment. He was the perfect travel partner for a paranoid amateur who, more than once on this journey, would show every opposite characteristic.

The day we ran was freezing and windy. I remember having an energy gel pack in my pocket and within minutes it was frozen solid as a rock. The temperature was around negative thirty degrees with head winds that were so strong on the back side of the six-mile loop that they pushed our bodies around like tumbleweeds in an Arizona windstorm. It was horrible and brutal—and this was only marathon number one.

As I was running on the ice, I noticed a man who was watching us run. One lonely man was brave enough to stand and cheer us on; we had one solitary fan on this remote landmass called Antarctica. He yelled out, "Don't worry about going fast; just keep gaining ground." In other words, "Just keep taking one small step at a time." One small step adds up over time to many. Much to my surprise, I finished that marathon, running on a glacier, in less than five hours. Our one-man cheering section had given me an awesome sermon about the value of one step at a time.

> One small step adds up over time to many.

The plane arriving to pick us up flew over us as we were still running. It could not risk being parked for very long in the cold, so we went into a tent, ate Mexican food (which was shockingly amazing) and headed back to Chile for our second continent run in South America.

Chile was perfect! The weather was a cool fifty degrees, and I was glad to see that I could loosen up to run the second marathon. The general rule in running is that after a marathon you should take 26 days off to rest, one rest day for every mile you ran. That was not happening here. I learned that momentum is an incredible thing, because it carried me through the race and I exceeded expectations by running it in less than four and half hours. The only regret I had about it was that before the race I had wanted to run at least one marathon in under four hours, and the conditions there were perfect to do it, but something in me told me to hold back, which I think was a mistake. I should have seized the moment—one of those rare moments where the wind is at your back. I find it interesting to see how great at running against the wind we can become, only to hold back when we have an opportunity to do something great, expecting the worst around the corner.

So I missed my chance to do a race in under four hours, but it was still a wonderful experience. I will never forget running along the water where the locals from the city cheered us on and brought us baked foods from their homes. One woman gave us patches in honor of our accomplishment.

The postmarathon routine was you finish, you eat, you head to the airplane. From that moment on, reality set in. I would never feel remotely normal again. Pain, pain, pain. I slept for maybe ten hours in all seven days put together. I am naturally a light sleeper, so the idea of sleeping with legs elevated to avoid blood clots was not very thrilling.

The wheels touched down, and we arrived in Miami. This is where I discovered how far love can carry someone. I had one advantage in Miami that no one else had. I had friends and family who cheered me on and encouraged me. When I was running in Miami my brain was in this strange kind of fog that was slowing my reaction time to everything. Mental fatigue is a real thing—but so is encouragement. People showed up to help me. Pastors flew in just to run next to me, as well as family and friends. Every mile someone ran with me, splashing me with cold water with every step I took in the hot Miami sunshine. Along the beach path friends lined the road giving me food. From the sidelines, my wife and kids were calling me their hero. Every word of encouragement was like a string of diamonds. My every step was empowered by lavish love.

Friends and family can help you perform at a higher level. They charge the environment with hope, which allows even the underdog to come out as a winner. They create an environment that will not let you fail.

Words of encouragement are always more powerful than you think. In Miami, they lifted me to the finish line, and I'm sure I performed beyond my potential. The encouragement felt supernatural. No other runner had what I had—the home court advantage. Not only was I on home soil, but for the first time, I realized something very real—friends and family can help you perform at a higher level. They charge the environment with hope, which allows even the underdog to come out as a winner. They create an environment that will not let you fail.

Home Court Advantage

I would like to challenge you to create a home court advantage for those you love. When your kids come home from a stressful school day, make your home a refuge. When they see your car parked outside, may they take a deep breath of relief because no matter what they have just gone through, they know they have the home court advantage of a supporting family. Businesses can achieve a home court advantage when their environment is so encouraging that when you just walk in the door, you can feel the hope and optimism. In a supportive environment, people feel safe and free to flourish.

This is the one thing we have tried do at the Dream Center: to create a place where people trapped in impossible circumstances for the first time feel that they have no choice but to win because they are surrounded by people with great expectations.

I think the thing that inspired me most about this marathon journey was the power of kindness. You have heard the phrase "death by a thousand cuts"? Well, this journey was fueled by people who displayed a thousand acts of kindness.

A man named Jonathon Fischer was a prime example. He was the one guy who came prepared during the World Marathon Challenge. He had everything! He had a leg compressor recovery machine; he had all the latest rolling devices for sore muscles, healthy energy drinks and the best snacks. When we completed a marathon, he would walk the aisles of the old private plane we flew in, sharing his stuff with everyone. He was the greatest joy of the journey by far. We all fell in love with this guy. He knew the power of one small act of kindness and how far it could go.

Marathon as Metaphor

We landed in Madrid, Spain, for marathon four. We were walking on water and doing amazing things, but we did not have the time to stop and appreciate our feat. This is where it all changed. At mile six a sharp pain developed in my knee. It was so sharp that I knew something was wrong instantly. I stopped at the checkpoint so it could be examined and discovered that it was a partial tear in my patellar tendon.

The first thing I thought was, *This is over.* I thought about all the people I was about to let down back in Los Angeles, the cheering army of people who had sent me off on this trip and who were using my race as a metaphor for their own journeys. They told me that if I finished the race, they would know they could finish their own races and get through rehabilitation. They were living through my journey.

But how could I go on? The doctor who traveled with us told me it was best to just stop and that there was no way to finish the rest of the races. Then, I realized something. What do you do when there is no one around to encourage you? You pull yourself together, and you *encourage yourself.* That is what David did when his life was under threat of death. "David encouraged himself in the LORD" (1 Samuel 30:6 KJV). He found a way to keep going.

I also learned that you need to let yourself break down in order to find your breakthrough. When I heard what the doctor said about my injury, I stopped and cried until I could cry no more. I had not broken down and cried like that for years. You can go from one achievement to the next and never allow yourself to just have a good cry. The circumstances were horrible, but in a bizarre kind of way, it felt good to just weep. Tears allowed me to somehow dream again, midrace. This expression of vulnerability proved to be helpful not just because it got emotions out of me that needed to be expressed, but because at the end of my tears I found a solution.

> You need to let yourself break down in order to find your breakthrough.

When I came to the end of myself, somehow I became capable of rebuilding myself through self-encouragement. I decided to lock my leg and use the other muscles in my leg to propel me. Maybe I could finish a marathon with a locked leg, and the other parts of my body would rise to the occasion to compensate. Somehow it worked, and I finished marathon number four limping all the way to the finish line. Completing marathon number four was shocking to me and those around me. It felt like a surprising accomplishment to finish on a high note of at least getting through four out of seven.

My journey was over. I was planning to fly back to Los Angeles. After the race, all the runners went to a little restaurant next to the park where we had run. The runners wished me well in my journey of life, and I said good-bye to all of my new international friends. I called the airlines to book a flight home. That is when I felt God's heart speaking to me, *Just give Me one more marathon.* (God has been playing that merciful trick on me for decades in ministry. *Just give Me one more day, one more act of love.* It keeps me around long enough to transition from near-death to stability and then back to life.)

Many times in life we think it is over, only for God to do something brand-new to let us know it has just begun. I hobbled to the bus that was about to leave and said, "Hold on! I'm going to take a few more steps and go with you guys. Who knows; maybe there is a way to grind out one more marathon."

I have learned in life that you have got to put yourself in a position where you need a miracle in order to receive it. I was about to need one.

MY SMALL STEP 2

After reading about this step and taking some time to pray, write down the small step you will take to follow God's nudge.

STEP 3

The Steps You Think You Cannot Take

Have you ever said yes when God was asking you to do something difficult, thinking that He was about to reward you with something incredible? That is what I thought when we touched down to run marathon number five in Morocco, on the continent of Africa. Every eager runner who had been filled with such joy at the start of this challenge now looked like a zombie from *Night of the Living Dead*. We all knew we were doing something incredible, but none of us had the energy to celebrate it.

We received the best news that we had heard yet on the trip. A temporary hotel stay had been granted and every runner would get four hours to rest. I felt like the people on the TV show *Survivor* when the host walks in to give them food or a small prize for their perseverance. I remember walking into that hotel room and in one motion throwing my bag to the side while falling into the bed. I slept for one hour! I woke up and took a shower. Then I went through my roommate's goodie bag on the floor to get some of his food stash. He was asleep so I figured he would not know or care. It was four hours of bliss! I never knew how valuable rest could be.

I had it all figured out—God wanted me to do one more marathon because He was going to heal me and do an extraordinary miracle. The vision in my head played out like *Forrest Gump*. You remember the scene where he took off running and his leg braces fell off? Yep, that is what I thought was going to happen.

Wrong! The gun went off, and I started to run—and fell flat on my face because of the pain and leg weakness. My tendon felt ten times worse, like a stretched-out accordion. I crawled to my feet, a bit mad at God for giving me the spontaneous courage to go on, only to forsake me in Morocco.

A friend of mine from Los Angeles named Justin Verduyn had raised money to fly to Morocco and run with me in Morocco and Dubai. His presence cheered me on; it was one more amazing act of love poured out on me during this journey. However, I was a bit disappointed that he had spent all this money to run with me only to join Pastor Limp-Along on his uninspiring run of trying to drag himself to the finish line.

Feeling hopeless, I looked up, and God gave me an answer to the puzzle of getting to the finish line while enduring this much pain. There were lampposts lining the marathon route every fifty yards. Glancing at them, I felt that God was giving me a strategy for how to run injured. My plan was to walk as far as one lamppost and then try to jog to the next one, without even thinking about how far I had to go. I turned off my GPS mileage-counting watch and kept my eyes on the closest lamppost. "One Lamppost at a Time" would be the mantra. The vision was not one of accomplishment but rather of courage.

I found out that when your dreams in life die, you can nevertheless maintain the dream of staying courageous. You can inspire more people by limping to your future than you can when everything you touch seems to turn to gold. Walk when you can, jog when you can, but stay courageous. Learn to find joy in effort and grit. Faithfulness carries with it a built-in reward. God is not impressed with our success; He is impressed with our ability to grow inwardly when life on the outside seems to be caving in. You please God by worshiping Him with whatever you have left to give Him. Your life circumstances are outside of your control, but you can control one thing: You can maintain a heroic heart. It is incredible how far you can go when you are not worrying about the distance you need to travel.

> When your dreams in life die, you can nevertheless maintain the dream of staying courageous.

One lamppost at a time. Fifty yards at a time. I made it to the end.

This was a reflection of my entire life, which has been filled with one victory at a time. One room at the Dream Center was occupied when that is all we had the money to renovate; one more family was rescued off the street. I believe that the secret to consistent growth is learning to celebrate the small wins of life and the little steps of progress. Most people quit because they fail to appreciate small steps of progress.

From that race to the present time, those lampposts have been a constant inspiration for me.

Skip the Applause

I limped to the finish line in Morocco, stunned at how far small steps can take you. I had always said to others, "One step at a time!" as an encouraging phrase, but now I knew that it truly works.

At the end of races one through four, there had been a cheering crowd that met the runners at the finish line. But this time my pace was so slow that there was no crowd to cheer for me at the end. Is that not a picture of life, as well? People cannot be your source of encouragement, because sometimes they will be there for you and sometimes they are nowhere to be found. No applause was necessary, anyway. Simply getting to the end produced its own reward.

When I was a young pastor chasing success, I could only celebrate the outward appearance of victory. Growing older, I have learned to appreciate victories of the heart, the wins no one else can see. Crossing the finish line in Morocco and seeing no cheering fans reminded me of the beauty of celebrating grit and determination and giving it back to God as an act of worship.

Can I encourage you to celebrate victories of the heart? When you defeat anger, do not stop at telling yourself "That's just what I'm supposed to do," pushing celebration aside. Rejoice! You have just won a battle you lost in the past. Celebrate growth! We do not do it often enough. We make a big deal about our failures, but very rarely do we encourage ourselves after we win. Thus we fall for the enemy's lie that our failures are a big deal and our victories do not matter. The greatest wins in life involve overcoming a limiting belief about your own self. I think that the older we get, the more we value these hidden victories.

> The greatest wins in life involve overcoming a limiting belief about your own self.

Pump your fist in the air when you win a challenge! Give yourself the momentum to succeed. Let God love you and celebrate with you.

Barefoot with Blisters

Now reality set in: "I've got two more to go. I might as well finish." The two biggest barriers now to reaching the finish line were not only the excruciating pain but also time. We had only eight hours to complete each marathon, and my body would not allow me to run that fast. We landed on continent number six—Asia—the nation of Dubai. Honestly, I never knew Dubai was on the continent of Asia. (I needed a serious geography course before this challenge.)

The course in Dubai was a rubber track along the beach. It was a strange surface to run on, but it did not make any difference one way or the other to all the pain. Now my compensating muscles, such as my hips and calves, were in agony. Everything was hurting. I had to take off my shoes and put them on the side of the track because the back part of the shoe was jamming into my Achilles tendon, which felt like a rubber band about to snap. Without sounding overly spiritual, it did feel as though God was holding the injured tendon together by His merciful hand. I kept thinking, "It's about to snap!" But it just hung by a thread—much like this entire race.

So I was forced to run barefoot. Normally, something like blisters would cause too much pain to keep running, but because I had so much pain everywhere, I hardly noticed my feet. It was just warm enough in Dubai to lightly heat up the track surface. That was certainly hot enough to cause pure torture to my puffed-up, blistered feet. The options were bad either way: Put pressure on the wrecked Achilles tendon or walk on blisters. To run 26 miles barefoot with blisters was the least of my concerns, as my body had forsaken me in every possible way.

I was walking, jogging, limping my way along when I looked at my watch and realized I was not going to make it. I had fallen too far behind to make it in under eight hours. Then suddenly, a man I had never met who lives in Dubai showed up on the scene. He was a businessman who lives two weeks a month in Dubai and two weeks a month in London. He had been following my journey on social media and decided I needed help. The Spirit of God had told this man to come and pay me a visit. He was like an angel who appeared by my side as I was struggling even to limp. He said, "Can I join you?"

I said, "Yes, but it won't be long. I'm not sure I can make it." This guy tended to every need that I had. He was not planning on doing a marathon that day, but he ended up doing one. This happened a few times on this trip. Random people showed up to walk a mile with me, and they ended up completing their first marathon.

This running saint got me anything I needed. He was of South African descent and had played rugby in his country, so he knew how to stretch my muscles. He gave me a sports massage just to try to wring one more mile out of me. He was so kind and so caring that I thought he was an angel. I might have been loopy from going crazy in the hot sun, but his act of compassion touched me deeply. He was with me until the end of the race. He talked about ministry things that took my mind off how badly I hurt. I think he wore a smile for the whole twenty miles he was with me.

God has provision ready for those who refuse to give up, who just keep taking the next step.

This is how I learned another valuable lesson on this journey: When you have done all that you can do, God will send you angels of mercy—if you just keep walking. God has provision ready for those who refuse to give up, who just keep taking the next step. This reminds me of Hebrews 10:36, which reads, "You need to persevere so that when you have done the will of God, you will receive what he has promised."

The prize is always at the end of enduring. Hang around long enough to see them. Miracles always seem to find those who are obedient and courageous. God shows up when He sees your endurance and struggle and He loves to help. This man was my reward for persevering, a reminder that good things happen if you just keep going. He actually carried me to the finish line with his encouragement.

Together, we finished in Dubai in only a few minutes under eight hours. This was good! However, I had used up every minute of my time; the bad part was that there was no time to take a shower or to eat. The penalty for running at such a slow pace was having little time to recover.

Adding insult to injury, someone had stolen my shoes that I placed on the side of the road, and it appeared that I would need to board the plane shoeless. (My extra shoes were in my suitcase, already loaded inside the baggage hold.) Mike Wardian had finished his marathon in a swift two and three-quarter hours. He saw me shoeless and said, "You can have these slippers they gave me at the spa." (He was so fast that he had time to go to the spa. I wanted to slap him for being such a fast runner, but I also wanted to hug him for giving me the slippers.)

Quickly, I put on the slippers. I had to get on the plane for the final continent, Australia.

Breakdown before Breakthrough

There was a certain kind of joy on the plane flying to Australia. People felt close to accomplishing their goal and a new surge of momentum filled the cabin. Everyone seemed to get a portion of their energy and vitality back. We could almost see the finish line; we had to make only one final surge. The ups and downs of our challenging marathons had made the victory sweeter.

Almost everyone on that plane felt that the last marathon was like a victory lap. They were writing letters to themselves and families about what the trip meant to them. Some were throwing a party, knowing by this point they had made it through the hardest part of their grueling test.

Almost everyone. Not me. My pain was escalating. No shower, no shoes. It gave me scant encouragement to think that sometimes right before the biggest victories there will be one last hurdle to overcome.

On the flight from Dubai to Australia I fell asleep for three hours, only to wake up to a rapid heartbeat. It felt like my heart was trying to break loose from my body. I woke up, light-headed, with my heart beating so strongly that I was certain I was going to die. There was no doubt in my mind. The other runners rushed to assist me and to settle me down. I remember looking at the picture of the flight map and all it showed was eight more hours of flying with no land in sight. A tragic feeling of hopelessness filled my soul as I realized there was no place to land this plane. The only thing I could do was to take as many deep breaths as possible, hoping to calm down.

When you feel you are going to die, it is amazing how much more you fall in love with the people you already love. I thought about my family, who had warned me about this dangerous undertaking. I decided to write good-bye letters to my family. I thought, *If I pass away, my legacy will be going out doing something ridiculous, and I will leave behind such a precious family. . . .*

My heart kept pounding in my chest until we landed in Australia. They escorted me off the plane and took me immediately to a hospital near Sydney. Thankfully, it was a slow night, and the doctor took me in quickly. He asked me questions about why I was in this condition, and to be honest, I did not want to tell him, because what I was doing seemed so reckless and irresponsible. The last thing I needed right now was a lecture. I had to tell him my medical history, about the blood clots and running such an extreme set of races in spite of that.

The doctor did not judge me. Instead he told me he thought it was awesome and that I needed to continue. He went a step further and told me that the pain of regret of not finishing my final marathon would be worse than the suffering I was going through and he was going to do whatever he could to get me on course to run the final marathon.

I could not believe it—a doctor was telling me to throw caution to the wind and finish what I started. He was an angel of motivation coming to my side. "Play it safe" was *not* his motto. I have never had so much treatment done in such a short time. It felt like NASCAR—going through a quick tune-up to be sent out immediately onto the speedway. He completed several tests and found that I had suffered a heatstroke along with a pain-related, stress-related panic attack. I had always heard people talk about panic attacks, and in my ignorance, I had thought they were no big deal. Boy, was I wrong. This experience gave me so much sympathy for those facing panic attacks and other anxiety-related ailments.

The final scene: four o'clock in the morning. I came straight from the hospital to the start line of the final marathon in Australia. The plastic wristband from the hospital was still around my wrist, and I was peeling off adhesive stickers that had attached the electrodes to my skin. I had to start the race later than the others, but we had a little more time on the clock to finish because we had banked extra time in our travel. The other runners were shocked to see me on the course and gave me high fives along the way. Mike Wardian ran the entire race dressed up like Elvis, and his crazy antics put a smile on my face.

I went from thinking I was going to die to a jubilant crossing of the finish line. As I crossed the finish line, they put an American flag over my shoulders and then placed all nine medals around my neck: one for each continent and two more for being a part of an exclusive club. Best of all, we raised an astonishing $1.4 million for the Dream Center's outreach programs. If I had stopped at marathon four, only $300,000 would have been raised. On top of that, people were inspired. With me, they learned that if you refuse to stop, you will be in a situation where God can resurrect you.

> The miracle is always in the next step you cannot take.

The miracle is always in the next step you cannot take. The Scripture we most commonly quote from the Bible is Philippians 4:13—"I can do all things through Christ who strengthens me" (NKJV). It is a great verse, but it means a lot more when you attempt something that is greater than your ability, something that requires God to take you beyond your human willpower or human strength.

Take the Impossible Step

If right now you are struggling to take one more step, do it anyway! Miracles are beyond the ordinary and the predictable. Miracles crash through quitting points. Believe for the impossible. What is the step you think you cannot take? Take it! And consider going the extra mile, where you might be blessed to see the beauty of an unfamiliar path. With God's help, you will be able to rise to the level of your challenge. Never be afraid to do something that is bigger than you are.

One final thing. Not only will God give you the courage to finish what you have started, but sometimes He will also give you little bonuses you do not even need, simply because He loves you. God is loving and so wonderful that He will often grant you the whispers of your heart. Here is what happened: I was never a great athlete as a kid, but my dream was always to be on ESPN's "Plays of the Day." At the end of each sports news show, they replay the best highlights of the day across all sports. Usually, it is a basketball slam dunk, a mammoth baseball home run that flies out of the stadium or a diving catch in the outfield.

ESPN requested video of me and Mike Wardian finishing the World Marathon Challenge. I could understand why they would want Mike, because he ran every marathon in less than three hours and broke all kinds of records. But why would they want footage of a guy who could barely walk? That would be the most boring thing to watch on television. That evening on "Plays of the Day" they showed Mike Wardian crushing records and Pastor Limp-Along fighting for every step. They mentioned my injury and how I made it to the end. Evidently, both of us could be considered champions: the one who limps to the finish line and the one who puts on an extraordinary show. What a gift!

> Keep taking the steps you do not think you can take, and God will give you the power you need. He might even shine on you a little extra something that can only come to the courageous of heart.

Not only had God given me the courage to finish the race, but He had also decided to fulfill a childhood wish that was not important in the grand scale of things.

Keep on keeping on! Keep taking the steps you do not think you can take, and God will give you the power you need. He might even shine on you a little extra something that can only come to the courageous of heart.

MY SMALL STEP 3

After reading about this step and taking some time to pray, write down the small step you will take to follow God's nudge.

STEP 4

Make Everything a Big Deal

One of the great secrets behind the success of the Dream Center has always been celebrating small steps. Here, we think celebration is a big deal. People's journey back from devastation and bad choices can seem overwhelming, to the point that trying may feel pointless. But by celebrating tiny steps of progress, we can keep guilt and condemnation away. Celebration keeps hope and joy alive. A person who has lost everything needs to know that any progress is worth throwing a party for.

At every church service, I invite someone whose life has been impacted at the Dream Center to give a testimony. Sometimes people think I am crazy because I will allow someone who has been clean from drugs for only two weeks to give a testimony. Their argument is that they are not "proven" yet. Still, I believe that for some people two weeks of being sober is major progress, and it needs to be celebrated.

My grandmother used to say, "You get what you brag on," and there is truth in that. When progress with your teenagers seems elusive, it is important for you as a parent to tell your kids how much you value the little things they do right. Make a big deal of it. You can rant and rave about the D your daughter got on her report card and completely miss the A. The D needs to be dealt with, but the A needs to be celebrated. People need to feel loved and inspired—even our own kids.

It bothers me how often, in times of trial, we will elevate a crisis and spend hours dealing with it. We will talk endlessly about a crisis, and we will allow navigating through it to eat up large chunks of everyone's time. However, when something good happens, we tend to give it only a brief recognition. Our culture seems to have an unhealthy attachment to bad news and very little appetite for good news.

> Trials become easier to manage when you have learned to be thankful for your incremental progress, and seeing how far you have come gives you courage to face whatever is next.

Crisis management is not the secret to sustaining a dream, learning to celebrate growth (at any level) is. Trials become easier to manage when you have learned to be thankful for your incremental progress, and seeing how far you have come gives you courage to face whatever is next. I cannot emphasize it too much: Making a big deal about small victories is the secret to successfully handling problems down the road.

Running the Race of Life

Anyone who knows me knows how much I love the sport of track and field. I especially love the storylines around the sport. My daughter is one of the top high-school milers in the nation, and watching her run brings me such joy.

It was a typical Saturday track meet where my daughter's club team, the Los Angeles Falcons, was taking on other junior kids' track teams. At the last minute, they needed a volunteer to help with the races. They asked me to line up the younger kids so they would be ready for the next race. The cute third- and fourth-grade runners got their little race bibs on and were sitting down waiting for their 100-meter race. Some of the kids really wanted to be there, while others were only going through the motions because their parents wanted them to be there. Trying to hype the kids up, I said "You're going to do awesome!"

Looking down the line, I noticed one kid who was holding his stomach. I asked, "Are you okay?" He said, "I'm feeling really sick. I haven't had anything to eat for a long time." I looked down at his tennis shoes and saw that half of each sole had holes. I could not see how he could even run in them. I thought about my daughter and the new spikes she was wearing and the carb-loaded meal she had eaten the night before to prepare. And here was this precious young boy who had everything working against him. I said, "Hold on for a second. . . . I'm going to get you something." I ran to the snack bar and got a cup of fruit and hurried back to give it to him. A strange idea came over me to make a big deal about this cup of fruit. I told him, "This isn't just a cup of fruit. This is a superpower cup of fruit. It is so powerful that when you run you're going to break your all-time record." He looked at me, curious about why I was making such a big deal about a cup of fruit, but then he gobbled it down quickly.

He ran the race and finished third. I asked, "What was your time?"

Proudly he put his shoulders back and said, "My best time ever." I am sure the cup of fruit helped this hungry boy, but I think making a big deal about his life and his race was the bigger fuel that kept him going. Upon hearing the news of his record, I jumped up and down, and the young man's face lit up. I told him, "Now that the race is over, I'm going to buy you a high-powered hot dog and chips." (Okay, maybe I took the analogy a little too far. But you get the point—making a big deal about people's progress is all-important.)

Jesus did that. He made a big deal about little things. He celebrated the widow's mite, which was not a big gift but rather a great act of courage (see Mark 12:41–44 and Luke 21:1–4). Then there was the centurion who asked Jesus to just say the word so that his servant could be healed from a distance (see Luke 7:6–9). He did not feel worthy to have Jesus in his home, but he knew Jesus could do a miracle from afar. This declaration of faith pleased Jesus so much that He made an incredible statement to the crowd: "I tell you, I have not found such great faith, even in Israel" (verse 9). Jesus made a big deal about the man's faith. Jesus understood how to make much out of a thing that others would feel was minor.

> I want to live a life of thanksgiving and never feel entitled to anything.

I travel a lot and speak at churches, and many times when I arrive at the hotel, I will find a gift basket in the room. Every time I receive one of those, I go out of my way to tell the church how much it means to me. I want to live a life of thanksgiving and never feel entitled to anything.

Celebrate Each Step

When I first came to Los Angeles to pastor the church at twenty years of age, every small step of progress felt impossible. Daily I felt as though I was walking in deep, thick quicksand. Most of the people in the congregation that I had inherited were over eighty years of age, and the ones I was starting to bring to church were from homeless encampments, riding the buses from skid row. As a pastor, I felt surrounded by the kind of rough men who came to King David when he was hiding in the cave from an angry King Saul.

A businessman showed up, and he became the first congregation member who had some money. He told me he was so moved by the sermon that he wanted to support the vision, and he handed me a $2,500 check. When I saw it, I almost fainted in disbelief. Before that, the offerings had consisted of one-dollar bills and loose change; to get a check like that was overwhelming. I called my dad on the phone to tell him the good news. At that time my dad was the pastor of one of the largest churches in America, and over the years he had received many large checks of a much greater magnitude. However, he was wise, and he understood the power of momentum. I will never forget his response. He said, "No way! This is the most incredible news I could hear." He added, "I'm going to fly out from Phoenix to Los Angeles just so we can celebrate that miracle."

Looking back at this, it seems funny. In the two decades since then, we have received five gifts to the Dream Center of over one million dollars each. Financial miracles have fallen like rain from heaven. We have been in situations when the power was about to be turned off and someone showed up with a check on a Friday afternoon to keep the lights on. My dad was making a huge deal about a $2,500 gift from a plumber in the church.

He bought a ticket with his own money and landed in Los Angeles on a Sunday night after speaking twice at his church in Phoenix. I picked him up at the airport, and we went straight to a greasy old steak place downtown called The Pantry. Throughout the entire meal he just kept saying, over and over, "Isn't God so good?" One of the most successful pastors of our generation was making a big deal about the offering given to his twenty-year-old son who was struggling to survive one more day in his urban church plant.

Two things happened there. A check from a businessman kept me in the call of God for a few more weeks, and a seasoned pastor flew out to have a victory party because of it. Both acts of kindness poured life into my veins.

Making a big deal about small steps creates momentum in a world full of fatigue. These two gracious acts kept me from quitting the ministry. They reminded me that there is more for me in going forward than in looking back. They reminded me to do the same thing for others. How many people are close to taking a life-changing step if only someone with the heartbeat of an encourager will make a step of faith toward them? A simple text message that says "I love you" can become a defining moment.

> Making a big deal about small steps creates momentum in a world full of fatigue.

Responders vs. Floaters

Life is about living as a responder rather than as a floater. A responder looks for a way to become a turning point in another's life. A floater waits until circumstances magically appear that bring happiness. A responder finds happiness in little things and decides to be a giver. A floater waits until life happens and lets circumstances shape what he or she believes. God wants us to steward our lives, taking charge of our happiness by letting abundance and gratitude flow from our hearts. By learning to follow God's nudge to do what is good and right, we are to live in such a way that we create life-giving experiences wherever we go. God is provoking us all the time toward good works, and we should challenge others to do the same.

I can see why so many pastors leave the ministry early. We can call it burnout, but I believe that it comes from forgetting the simplicity and joy of doing what we get to do. When we first start preaching, we are so nervous that our light is on all night long as we pray and ask God for help. Everything is new, and therefore everything is alive. The years go by, and we get better at preaching. The things that brought so much excitement before no longer feel like a big deal. We fall into the sin of getting used to it. We may get to the point where we cannot even enjoy the victories anymore because we are so accustomed to the common blessings of God.

We need to get our celebration back. Celebration develops the perspective that the blessings of God are just as great now as the first time we experienced them. I know some of the richest people in the world, but they cannot enjoy what they have because they have become used to what they have. God wants His Church to be people of celebration.

I love to watch a ball game and see a kid who never gets to play get sent in by the coach in the last minute of a blowout game. He runs onto the court and is so excited to play that he forgets his position, forgets his assignment on who to guard and forgets everything in his joyful passion. He runs around, ecstatic to have been called into the game, so happy to be chosen. Most people who burn out in the ministry forget their first joy of just being on God's team. Childlike thrill is replaced by obligation. The water cooler at work, where you used to see opportunities to witness or encourage others, now feels like a place you want to avoid.

I know what I'm talking about because I do it myself. When church is over on a Sunday, my mind goes to seven days down the road rather than the victory we just experienced. It is one of my greatest weaknesses—my attention is always somewhere in the future, and I fail to throw a victory party in the present. Lately I have been exploring this part of my life. The call of God and grunting it out have kept me going for 25 years, but *celebration* will keep me fueled for the next 25 years.

Celebrate!

Make it a practice to celebrate things you have overlooked in the past. The Bible says, "In the same way, I tell you, there is rejoicing in the presence of the angels of God over one sinner who repents" (Luke 15:10). A perfect heaven is celebrating the repentance of a flawed sinner. Heaven is making a big deal about one person's right decision. In the same way, we need to make a big deal about one another's victories and successes.

The best thing to do while waiting for your own victory is to celebrate other people's victories. Celebration cultivates a life of faith and it leaves a powerful legacy. I am not talking about simply being positive, but about being Spirit-led, looking for opportunities to pour out your life, deciding not to accumulate burdens. Naturally, you will have burdens; burdens are part of the reality of life. But even the burdens feel lighter when you are serving others, and your actions will not add to the burdens. Jesus says:

> Come to me, all you who are weary and burdened, and I will give you rest. Take my yoke upon you and learn from me, for I am gentle and humble in heart, and you will find rest for your souls. For my yoke is easy and my burden is light.
>
> Matthew 11:28–30

Give when you need someone to give to you. Inspire other people's dreams while waiting for someone to inspire yours. Pat someone else on the back when life is giving you a kick in the pants. That is how you can take your life back and live it from a new place. The truth is, of course, that this kind of life means you have to go out of your way and break your comfortable routines, and that is not easy. It is safer to exist rather than to live this way. Existing is also like a slow death. When we mistake existing for living (and giving), our lives become spiritless. We die slowly and we cannot tell what is happening. The Bible describes this kind of life: "But she that liveth in pleasure is dead while she liveth" (1 Timothy 5:6 KJV). This Scripture is admonishing a widow who is seeking worldly things to make her happy; it emphasizes the emptiness of living for ourselves. We will always feel the most fulfilled when we are the most poured out.

> The best thing to do while waiting for your own victory is to celebrate other people's victories.

One day I was walking by a little park by our house and there was a Little League game going on. I had no idea who was playing, nor did I know anyone on the field. The game appeared intense, with fans cheering loudly. It seemed that the score was a close one, so I decided to watch the rest of the game. In right field, I noticed a young boy who has having a tough time. He had a hard time focusing and looked like he did not want to be there. Two balls went through his legs and rolled to the fence. With each ball that eluded his glove, I could hear groans from the fans. He was a liability to his team; this guy was clearly the player who was keeping the team from winning. I watched this boy for a while. It appeared to me that he was terrified; he did not want another ball hit his way. But sure enough, another ball did come his way, and once again it dropped between his trembling knees. The groans got louder, along with a few loud whispers about how this kid could not even come up with an easy grounder.

Out of nowhere I felt a nudge of the Holy Spirit. The nudge directed me to do something. I am sure this came from the Holy Spirit because there is no way my natural mind would even think of this. It was a strategy from heaven. The nudge was to become this kid's biggest fan. Whenever he did anything good, I should just start cheering for him. I did not know his name, so I called him Right Field. Right Field got up to bat and swung and missed. I yelled out, "Great swing, Right Field!" He looked up at me like, "Who is this crazy guy cheering for a swing and miss?" On the next pitch he hit a foul ball, and I yelled, "Great contact, Right Field." He struck out the next pitch and I yelled out, "That's a great swing on a tough pitch. No one could have hit that pitch." People were looking at me like I was loony. Right Field became my favorite player. In the next inning, they hit him a ball and he stopped it. (He did not catch it, but he stopped it.) I jumped up and down and said, "What a play, Right Field. Good job keeping the ball in front of you!" This young boy now had a fan base, an angel in the outfield. Honestly, I went wild from that point on, cheering for his warm-up, encouraging his hustle and finding joy in celebrating everything. Parents were looking at me, obviously thinking I was a lunatic; they did not share my passion for my new favorite player. I would like to say that Right Field made the game-winning hit because of the encouragement, but that did not happen. Still, something else happened, and it might be even more amazing—he played the rest of the game with a smile on his face. He had a fan, someone to celebrate him.

The world needs more fans who pull for those who have no cheerleader. *You* can do that. Why not decide to take the next step and make everything a big deal? Give yourself a permission slip and a free pass to enjoy life. Create a praise party everywhere you go and let life come out of you. Never get complacent. Look for reasons to rejoice, for there are many!

MY SMALL STEP 4

After reading about this step and taking some time to pray, write down the small step you will take to follow God's nudge.

STEP 5

The Small Steps
That Change Lives

I grew up in Phoenix, Arizona, the son of a megachurch pastor. The church of my father, Pastor Tommy Barnett, was one of the first to build a 6,500-seat auditorium, because the church had grown so much; an amazing ten thousand people were attending weekly.

As the son of a successful pastor, I was always scared to follow in his footsteps. It felt like a no-win proposition. If I succeeded, people would have expected it; if I did not, then they would have wondered why I was such a failure. My parents always thought there was something wrong with me growing up because I never talked. I was scared and shy. There really is no pathway to ministry for a young man who is scared of his own shadow.

Not that Dad failed to include me in things. When the church building was going up, he and Mom would take me over there every night to monitor the construction. I would go to bed late every night because of that. He was so excited, and he wanted to take me along for the journey. I explored every part of that building and even climbed up into the ceiling to the catwalks. (The church was one of the first churches to have cables so that people could "fly" in performances, such as Christmas plays. I even got to test the cables and soar through the sky like Peter Pan. Normally, Mom would never have allowed me to be the test pilot, but she had to keep a young boy entertained if she was going to take him to an empty building every night.)

The church had two balconies, and the ceiling was so high that when I looked up, I felt I was staring into the sky. On opening Sunday, the massive curtains opened, and the choir sang. There were so many people in attendance that some of them had to stand along the walls of the auditorium. Driving home from that historic day, we talked about the experience, and we knew from that day forward our lives would never be the same. *Time* magazine called the church one of the largest churches in America.

It appeared this development would be the catalyst to put a desire in my heart to follow in the footsteps of my father in ministry. It was not. How, then, did I end up serving in downtown Los Angeles? I am a megachurch pastor, but my church serves the forgotten people who live in cardboard boxes, the addict who cannot seem to get the needle out of his vein, the homeless family living in their car and so many others who need a second chance. It came about because of a simple and basic experience.

The week after my father opened that incredible building, he told me to be ready to wake up early on Sunday morning because he was going to drive down to the housing projects to pick up a family and bring them to church. I said to him, "Why? You're now the pastor of a megachurch, and you have a staff that can take care of that for you."

My dad just looked at me and said, "It's not about the crowds. It will always be about the one." He taught me that responsibility comes with influence, and success is worth having only if you reach down to the ones who have no one to fight for them. Dad's statement about serving "the one" pushed me over the edge of complacency, and the seed was sown in me for full-time ministry. The grand opening did not compel me to the ministry, it was the Sunday morning walk to the car to drive to the projects to transport a family to church.

You should have seen the look in the family's eyes when they realized that the man who was picking them up was the same man who was about to preach to 6,500 people in a three-story auditorium. When the service was over, my dad took this family to an all-you-can-eat restaurant; they were overwhelmed with his extra effort. They were so poor that they asked for several doggie bags to take home. I was more proud of my father's simple after-church kindness than I was of his message on that big stage.

Just One Small Step

It is amazing—you can take one single, ordinary step and to someone else it becomes a major catalyst for a life transition. Never discount the little things you do with a lot of love, because those can be the most powerful teaching moments for the next generation. I was a young pastor's kid who had seen it all. Nothing really impressed me. Yet there was just something about the purity of my father's simple act of driving to pick up a family when he was at the height of influence, and that is what called me into a life of full-time service to the people of Los Angeles.

When Neil Armstrong took one small step on the surface of the moon in 1969, he made a statement heard all over the word. "That's one small step for man, one giant leap for mankind." A little step can impact the world. When you follow the nudge to reach out to someone in a personal way, your action might seem so small. But others are following your example, and the simplicity of that moment is inspirational.

Truett Cathy, the owner of Chick-fil-A, once said, "We must motivate ourselves to do our very best, and by our example lead others to do their best as well." Of course we can give our best when the conditions are right, but it takes a person of character to do it when the conditions are not favorable. At times we have got to overcome our own pride to be a good example. When you put on a smile in order to make someone else's day, the world might call it hypocrisy for not being "true to yourself." But it is really a magnificent form of service when you would rather be served and have your ego stroked, and yet you give anyway. Selflessly, smile when you feel like frowning.

Do not listen to the world that tells you to be "you." Instead, be *better* than you—overcome how you feel and be the person God wants you to be. It is not always easy to be a good example, but people learn more in life from the little things you do than from the monumental moments. Serve others when you need to be served yourself. That is how you will reach the Ph.D. level of what it means to be a Christian.

A Most Generous Thank-You

Several years ago, the Dream Center started receiving very large monthly checks from a church in Memphis that was receiving a mission offering once a month just for us. We did not know anything about this place or anybody there; all we knew was that the checks were sent by the "World Overcomers Outreach." Early on, I called the church to ask to speak with the pastor to thank him, and the secretary responded, "Bishop Williams can't come to the phone right now because he's in meetings today. But he wasn't expecting any thanks. He was just obeying what God told him to do."

I hung up the phone. *How strange,* I thought. *He's giving this money, and he won't even take my call.* Years and years went by, and I could never reach him. Finally one day he decided to take my call. I went into my rapid-fire speech about how grateful we were and what his offering was doing to help our ministry. I was talking too fast because I had so much to say. He just listened.

When I finally let up to take a breath, he told me the reason for his monthly generosity. Bishop Alton Williams told me there was a time in his life when he was weary in the ministry, so he had attended our pastors' conference in Los Angeles at the Dream Center. My father and I had just finished a leadership session and were heading to the car for lunch. Bishop Williams shouted out to us in the parking lot and gave us a friendly wave. We stopped, waved back and went over to the car to talk to him. Then it turned into a brief time of prayer—five minutes. Five minutes! The impact and encouragement of that encounter was so profound upon his life that it kept him going in the ministry. His monthly offering was a big thank-you to us for going out of our way and taking five minutes to pray with him, as well as a seed offering to help the ministry of his church flourish with a heart for serving God and His people. The moral of this story is that we have no idea the level of fuel we carry to help others reach their dreams. The cause of our ministry is not what drove him to give; it was our spending just five minutes to pray for a servant of God who had become weary and needed to be strengthened in his inner man.

I think it would be a great idea after reading this chapter to create for yourself a five-minute challenge. For only five minutes every day for one month, go out of your way for others. You can spend that time praying for someone, buying a person a coffee, sending a long text of encouragement, making someone a song playlist or holding a door open for somebody who has a hard time walking. Whatever you feel led to do, let it be something outside your own routine. Just five minutes a day, let your mind run wild with compassion. Pay for somebody's gas, leave a nice note in your child's school lunch bag, warm up the car early on a cold day for your loved one. You could ask your church if they have a list of people in prison to whom you could send a quick letter of encouragement. You can change people's lives by stepping toward them in simple ways that can make them feel loved. And feeling loved can bring people back to life!

> Create for yourself a five-minute challenge. For only five minutes every day for one month, go out of your way for others.

Do Everything with Love

This very simple verse carries a lot of impact: "Let all that you do be done with love" (1 Corinthians 16:14 NKJV). Take charge of the battle that rages for your time and attention, and give love a chance. When you reach out to others in simple ways, you write little chapters in people's lives, footnotes in their stories.

People like Barnabas in the Bible did little things with a lot of love—and they were noted for it. Barnabas believed in Paul when no one would take a chance on him. People were afraid of the apostle

Paul, but not Barnabas—he was the one person to show him love. His support for Paul helped turn the world upside down. He could not preach like Paul, and he did not have natural leadership skills, but he stepped toward Paul with loving faith. One man's faithful encouragement became the springboard to a ministry that would inspire missionaries all over the world. Our small encouragements become like a cold glass of lemonade on a hot day, refreshing the world. Sometimes when we think that we are handing an olive branch to someone in need, we are really handing off a baton to carry a legacy forward.

In Los Angeles, the Dream Center is the place people usually call when they reach rock bottom. People say, "Go to the Dream Center. They'll take you." I take that statement as a compliment, not an insult. Police have driven people to the front door of our property in shackles and chains and asked us if we could take them. Judges have reduced sentences of prisoners, declaring, "Instead of jail you're going to the Dream Center rehab for one year." We have worked with drug-addicted pastors' kids as well as with ministry leaders who have fallen and need restoration. It is the greatest honor in the world to work

> Sometimes when we think that we are handing an olive branch to someone in need, we are really handing off a baton to carry a legacy forward.

with fallen people. We never justify the sin that brought people to our hospital, but we sure do have a fun time seeing dramatic comebacks and watching people get restored to God's dream for their lives.

My view of restoration is different from that of most others. When a pastor crashes in ministry or a person ends up at a place of destitution, they do not need a play-by-play description of everything they have done wrong. One of my pet peeves in ministry is the way pastors use someone's fall as an opportunity to teach a lesson about how that person fell, claiming that we can learn a moral lesson from hearing how it happened. People's failures are not Sunday school lessons! They are a reminder of how fast we must run to them in their time of need.

A huge part of restoration is the first few steps we take. Condemnation is a devastating weapon the enemy uses to tell someone why it is pointless even to try to rise again. To take steps that truly save people, we must overwhelm them with love and hope right after their biggest failures. We must cut off the cancer of condemnation before it starts to spread across a person's future. The enemy is not just after our present behavior; he wants to destroy our usefulness, our dreams and our fresh outlook about the future.

To counteract condemnation and despair, we unleash a saturation of hope immediately, when people are at their lowest point. In fact, we even ask people, "What is your dream?" right after they have fallen. We do not have all the answers as to why people fall short. The one thing we do know is this verse: "For all have sinned and fall short of the glory of God" (Romans 3:23). We know that there is a root of sin in all of us, and we will get to that root in the process of restoration. But we cannot dive into the root without giving people immediate hope. That is why it makes sense to ask, "What is your dream?" at a crisis point. When you ask this question to a broken person, the answer will usually be,

"Nothing." This answer is normal and to be expected, but by asking that question right away, you set the table. You are saying, "Anything is still possible." Even though it seems audacious and pointless to ask such a question, we ask it anyway!

Courage to Come Back

The Bible says, "Where there is no revelation, people cast off restraint; but blessed is the one who heeds wisdom's instruction" (Proverbs 29:18). Interestingly, vision and instruction go hand in hand. People need vision and they need guidance. Without vision, nobody has a reason to work on exercising restraint because living for something keeps you in the boundaries of what is right and what is wrong. At the same time, guidance keeps the vision on track. A fallen person needs someone else to step in with both. Right off the bat, vision helps kill the seed of condemnation that is threatening the fallen person. Vision sets the table for guidance. Discipline occurs after vision is restored. I have made it a point never to say to a broken person, "One day you'll dream again." Instead, I immediately establish a hope for the future. Discipline will follow where there is something to live for.

It might feel good to say, "I told you so," but it does not help anyone. Every month people come back who have failed our rehab program and left early. Their faces always look embarrassed; they failed the first time. I always make it a point to run up to them and make a big deal out of the fact that they had the courage to come back. I purposely make that one small step to say, "Forget about your failed first attempt. Let's give it another try." Instead of burying people in their pain (which is what the rest of the world wants to do), we want to be a bridge of hope that people can walk on toward their future. The world loves to mock those who have fallen, and sometimes the Church uses them as object lessons of what not to do. Instead, we champion the call to serve the most shamed in society. We want to demonstrate to the world just how far God's love can go and what it can accomplish—in anyone. Think about how Jesus was willing to put His reputation on the line for people who could give Him nothing in return.

Regularly, Jesus spent time with the kind of people about whom any publicist would say, "Don't get near that person! That person will be bad for your brand. You will gain nothing from being seen with that one. That loser will make you lose." Jesus moved toward people who were at rock bottom. He identified with the lowest of the low. If Jesus walked today, He would take selfies with these people on Instagram, and everyone would say, "He's ruining His life and sabotaging His career." Why would Jesus invest so much time with dysfunctional people who could do nothing to enhance His short, three-year span of public ministry? Jesus did not carefully craft His ministry career; He simply remained flexible about responding to the needs around Him:

> But made Himself of no reputation, taking the form of a bondservant, and coming in the likeness of men. And being found in appearance as a man, He humbled Himself and became obedient to the point of death, even the death of the cross.
>
> Philippians 2:7–8 NKJV

He made Himself of no reputation. This is not just God coming as Jesus in the form of human flesh, this is God loving everybody. Jesus lived a free kind of life. He had no unhealthy attachments or feeling of responsibility for explaining His level of kindness. Loving the underdog should not require an explanation. Like Jesus and with Him, we should strip ourselves of the meaningless quest to fit into the world's mold and never allow it to determine how we show God's grace to others.

Extra Steps of Grace

Reputation did not matter to Jesus because He was secure in His mission. Therefore, He could let it fly when it came to identifying with hurting people. Jesus did not just wait for hurting people to come to Him; He changed people's lives by going to them. It is one thing to be compassionate when people come to us for help; it is an entirely different level when we go out of our way to find people who feel they have no right to be loved. The incredible thing about our Savior was His complete willingness to go the extra mile, leave behind routine and take an extra step of grace. What He did was unprecedented and even baffling to the religious structure.

> It is one thing to be compassionate when people come to us for help; it is an entirely different level when we go out of our way to find people who feel they have no right to be loved.

We can take steps out of the way to change people's lives every day. You might be a teacher and you notice a kid who has no friends. You go out of your way to make that student feel important. You may be a student who simply sits by another student who has no friends in the lunch room. You may be a coach who encourages a player who drops the game-winning fly ball and tells him, "It's no big deal." Anytime we want to, we can reach out like this. We can live like Jesus and champion the cause of the underdog.

Many prisoners write me notes because they watch me on television, and sometimes I write them back. It floors me to see how thankful and shocked they are to get a response. The letters they send back to me always say so; they never expected me to respond. It is such a small thing to do. Acts of compassion that seem small to you give joy beyond comprehension to the forgotten. Closeness to Jesus can be achieved by bending low to help those in need.

I will admit that it is not easy to have an outreach church mingled together with a drive-in crowd. There have been times when I have wanted to scrap the bus ministry. It costs money, and sometimes we bring people to church who are drunk and they act out. In the middle of my sermon sometimes a drunk will come to the stage to shake my hand. We have lost people because of being that kind of church, but I would not change one thing. We will continue to bring them every Sunday morning.

The Gospel will always be edgy, and it always should involve inconvenience. The only steps that change people's lives are risky ones, the ones that are outside the norm, out of the way. At the end of the day, we are never acting more like Jesus than when we stop what we are doing and take a step toward the one who is in need.

MY SMALL STEP 5

After reading about this step and taking some time to pray, write down the small step you will take to follow God's nudge.

STEP 6

Step on Toes

Every parent understands the challenge of pushing your kids. We want them to dream and aspire to do great things, and we also want to make sure that they are doing things they love to do. However, sometimes we need to challenge them to move, to step out, to try something.

One Saturday night, I saw an ad promoting a local kids' track team in the community. My daughter was in eighth grade, and she would be eligible to join a youth team. She already played soccer and was a fast runner. In fact, she was so fast that when she would surge ahead with the ball, someone would always chop her legs down to stop her from scoring. I could see that her future in soccer would be filled with aches and pains.

I approached my daughter and said, "There's a track team starting and you can join and race tomorrow." I added, "You would be a great mile runner or a great two-mile runner. She looked at me like I was crazy. I kept saying, "Give it a try." We argued about it all evening. Finally I said, "I'll make a deal. If you run one race, I'll take you shopping at the mall tomorrow." She agreed. I picked the event: the 3,000-meter race against other eighth-grade boys and girls. The race would mean running seven and a half laps around the track. She was doing it for the shopping money, but I knew that once the race started her competitive instinct would kick in.

The gun went off, and her running power was a revelation. On her first race ever, she beat all the experienced boy and girls and almost set an all-time meet record. We went shopping after the race. Later she looked me in the eye and said, "Dad, I think I want to do another one." Since then, she has gone on to be one of the fastest high-school runners in the nation.

Step Up to the Challenge

Sometimes the small step that we need to take is to step on someone's toes, to challenge the other person to take a chance. This is exactly what Jesus did. He called out fishermen to be disciples; He called a shepherd boy to take on a giant; He called ordinary people to try extraordinary things. He is calling all of us personally to step up to challenges—and to challenge one another.

I never knew that one little shopping trip negotiation would lead to a career in running for my daughter and a Division 1 scholarship. She did not like me at the time, and the truth is she was mad at me all the way to the start line. But when you see something in another person, you have got to step past your hesitation and call out the greatness in them. We are not called so much to make others comfortable as we are to provoke greatness in them.

Sometimes it can create conflict. My wife, Caroline, is a remarkable communicator and public speaker. Yet every time I would ask her to speak, she would say no. One day from the pulpit I told the church, without telling her, "In two weeks my wife is going to speak." You talk about rough marital waters; for two weeks it was nasty. She did not want to talk to me, and she refused to believe that I had committed her to something she was not ready for. However, I knew she was ready, and I knew that she would hit a grand slam. I had to step on her toes a little bit, but it was worth it to have the gift of her teaching be imparted to the world. The Word of God tells us, "And let us consider one another to provoke unto love and to good works" (Hebrews 10:24 KJV). The Christian life is not just about telling people ways in which they need to change, but it is also challenging one another's potential.

Many Christians are great about keeping each other accountable about moral behavior, but sometimes we fail to challenge one another regarding our potential and faith to do more than we think we can do. The Dream Center has launched many preaching careers. I have been known to invite people to preach their first sermon to a crowd of two thousand people. Of course, it is risky to let your church be the one where people preach their first message. But it has allowed the Dream Center to become a safe cultivation ground for people to step out in faith.

> We should never be afraid to call out someone's potential, even if it means stepping on a few toes. We must create a culture of faith.

I think of all the people who have slipped through the cracks because their church did not have a forum in which they could share their gift. I believe the church should be a place where people get pushed out of the nest of safety and into the doorway of destiny. We should never be afraid to call out someone's potential, even if it means stepping on a few toes. We must create a culture of faith.

One day on Twitter, I came across a pastor named Chuck Balsamo. I had no frame of reference regarding his ministry; I just liked the guy. I liked his audacious way of living and his out-of-the-box thinking. One day God just said to me, "Invite him to preach." That was so out of the norm for me that I wondered if I made the right move. (He might have been a Twitter robot and not even a real person.) He turned out to be one of the greatest friends that the Dream Center has ever known. We challenge each other all the time and are not afraid to step on each other's toes.

Offended Pride

I have an honest confession: In the first ten years of my ministry, I was offended all the time by people who stepped on my toes. I took everything personally. My pride got in the way constantly. I would receive an email of criticism, and (I hate to say this) I would craft a message in which I would preach about the offense rather than forgiving or working something out. My offendedness was like ammunition for my sermons. That is a bad place to be: preparing sermons based on how mad you are versus preparing a sermon because you want to help people. It did not happen all the time, but too often my best-flowing ideas came out of my anger rather than a proper motivation. In other words, I could not handle a little criticism and critique.

Since then I have learned how little I know. Why should I get offended by criticism? Maybe I do not know everything after all. Now when I get critiqued, I look at it from two possible angles. If there is even a grain of truth in the criticism, I will use it to grow. If there is no truth and it is slanderous, I will try to make peace. This simple revelation set me free. Winning arguments is very overrated, and so is protecting one's own reputation. But learning something new or making a friend out of an enemy—now, that is living! My goal in life is not to be right but to be right with God.

Be the kind of person who is not afraid to call out greatness in people who do not see it in themselves, and be prepared to handle the challenge of people who might step on your toes. I know many people who are great at calling out greatness in others, but they have a hard time listening to critique when people step on their toes. Give encouragement, listen to critique and fight the urge to feel offended.

Keep Growing

The secret is to just keep growing all the time. Just try to get a little bit better every day. Stay hungry to learn. Look for nuggets of wisdom everywhere, even from impure vessels who might have only one percent of truth in what they say. If you can use that one percent to make you better—take it. Make up your mind that you will not take refuge in feeling hurt or remain stuck in victim mode.

One thing I love about my father is that, at 82 years of age, he is still growing. Things he used to be offended by no longer bother him. Throughout his life, he would repent to me and others, and he often told me how he felt he needed to change. He never led from perfection; he led from vulnerability. He would shock me when he would identify with my struggles by telling me he went through the same things. I found it hard to believe that my father could have dealt with the same temptations and struggles I was going through, and that encouraged me. By teaching his children about how he grew through his past mistakes, he avoided the parenting trap of portraying himself as a perfect kid who lived according to a higher standard "back in the day." Like most children, I did not need to see perfection in my parents, but I did need to see an example of growth.

I was invited to speak at my father's church in Phoenix on New Year's Day. When January 1 falls on a Sunday, that is not exactly the best day for church attendance. People have been up all night, and attendance usually plummets like a meteor from the sky on that day. Before the service, my dad took me to his favorite breakfast place— McDonald's. One of the little things I remember as a kid is going through the McDonald's drive-thru to get a sausage biscuit for breakfast. My dad would load that biscuit with a ridiculous amount of mustard, and one of the great joys of his life was that sausage biscuit. I am not kidding—he would even talk about it the night before.

We walked into McDonald's on this New Year's Sunday morning around seven thirty before the first service. My dad had a big smile on his face and said to the clerk at the front, "Give me a sausage biscuit." He walked over to the condiments section to get his five mustard packs and was all smiles. Anyone who knows my dad can visualize this; he gets very excited about the small things in life.

The man working the front looked tired, as if he really did not want to be there. You could see that he had been partying all night long. He called our number, and I went to get the food and brought it to our table. My dad unwrapped that paper like a child opening a present on Christmas Day. Sadly, it was *not* a sausage biscuit—it was an Egg McMuffin. His countenance dropped and he said, "They got me the wrong order."

I knew that in the past my dad never took well to people getting his food order wrong. I said, "I'll take it up and change it for you." He stopped and looked me in the eye and calmly said, "Son, don't take it up. I'll just eat it." I was completely stunned. They got his cherished sausage biscuit order wrong, and my father's face looked serene. Then he went on to say, "I've just decided today that I'm not going to grow up one day and be an old man who complains about everything." I wanted to laugh because he was old already, but at the same time I admired his ability to stay hungry not just for the sausage biscuit but for life. He was challenging himself, or you could even say he was stepping on his own toes. This seems like such a simple little story, but real growth happens by deciding to stay challenged and to keep stepping toward progress.

> Real growth happens by deciding to stay challenged and to keep stepping toward progress.

Faithful, Available, Teachable

The great thing about change is that you can decide at any moment to make progress. Think about an area you need to improve and just stop right now and say, "Is there any step I can take to face it head on?" When we decide to live in a faithful, available and teachable way, we can learn from every experience throughout every season of our lives.

I love to read about the disciples' lives and watch how they matured while they were with Jesus and then after Jesus ascended. When they were with Jesus, at times they were petty and small-minded, but after Jesus ascended, they were mission-minded.

A man once told me something that I thought was a cute little saying: "People change, but not much." I disagree. Hungry people change, and they change a lot. If we choose to live without offense, learning from the people who step on our toes who have good intentions (and even from those who criticize us with bad intentions), remaining completely teachable, we can, year by year, decade by decade, improve to become almost unrecognizable in the way we live.

I am writing this book one floor above where the men in our recovery program reside. I have seen some of these men change so drastically that after three or four years, I completely forgot they were ever in rehab. Every day for one year in the program, these men decide to get up and just try to get one percent better. Little by little, they change foundationally and quite miraculously. They become completely different. Their lives prove that people can grow and that they are not forever locked into the attributes and attitudes they started out with.

We are called to be people of growth, and one of the ways to grow is to let people step on our toes—even stepping on our own toes if there is no one else to do it. One thing I love about our church is that the more boldly I preach, the more they love it. The loudest shouts of "Amen!" I get from this motley group of misfits come from the sermon points that hit the hardest. The more I bring truth, the more excited they get. They have come to realize that correction is beautiful. When you have that approach to life, you do not bother to get offended because every day you are on an expedition to get better. Paul wrote to the church in Ephesus:

> You were taught, with regard to your former way of life, to put off your old self, which is being corrupted by its deceitful desires; to be made new in the attitude of your minds; and to put on the new self, created to be like God in true righteousness and holiness.
>
> Ephesians 4:22–24

Let's just say there is a drastic change depicted here in these verses. The corruption and deceit of the old nature transition into the new nature of holiness and pursuit of God. There is a very large gap between the two natures, but God would not allow such a big gap between what used to be and what we can be if it were not possible to bridge it.

Each day, be inspired by the gap, because real joy comes from seeing not how far you need to go but in taking the first step of the day. Just take one small step each day. Learn and grow; do not be condemned by how far you have got to go in any area of your life. Is there a challenge that you need to take on? Maybe you need to forgive someone or be nice to a person you have held a grudge against. The very fact that it is a barrier in your life means that it ought to be challenged.

Take That First Step

I cannot tell you how many dreams have been held back simply because the first step was never explored. At the same time, I have seen people never reach their potential because they had no one in their life to care enough to walk into their comfort zone and say, "You can do more."

It has been years since I have written a book, and to be honest with you, I thought my writing days were over. I kept telling myself that I would not write anymore. If you speak a lie over yourself for too long, you become paralyzed from even moving in the direction of faith. One day a man came up to me at church and said these words: "Just start," and then he walked away. It really was a strange encounter. No "Hello" or "How's it going?" He just walked up to me and said, "Just start."

I could not get those words out of my head. Start what? Maybe writing? So I decided to go to the computer and try to write something for just two hours. I put a timer on and said, "I'm going to try to write for two hours." Whatever I have after two hours is what I have. The words you read in chapter one of this book—"Since I was a child growing up in church, I have heard the phrase 'The dead coming back to life'"—those were the first few words that came to my mind, and they turned out to be quite fitting for this journey. By taking one small step, the words started to flow, and it really did feel like a dead part of me was coming back to life. The act of just sitting down and trying to write felt like the valley of dry bones when the resurrected bones started to become an army again.

Give life to your dreams by moving, and see where it takes you. Give life to the dreams of others by challenging them to believe for more. Step on your own toes, get yourself going, find yourself some friends who will challenge you to believe for more. Never stop moving, keep testing what is possible and, whatever you do, never be satisfied.

Change in Perspective

We must have people who will challenge our comfort zones not only when it pertains to our dreams but also when it pertains to our character. When I was a young pastor just trying to get going, I looked for every excuse why I could never build a great church in Los Angeles. There is too much crime. I am too young. Our building is too hard to find. I do not understand the culture. Huge limiting forces settled into my spirit that put my brain into a fog of containment. Excuses have power! I looked at my church that was surrounded by so much poverty, and I would say things like, "No one who could fund this church will drive to this part of town," or "You will never reach people without the proper church facilities." Those excuses became powerful, so that I started to believe that forward momentum was impossible. I came to expect defeat, and that is a terrible place to be.

Interestingly, when you start to look for the bad, you always find it. I would tell the church that I was hoping to make it one more week as their pastor. It is true that the challenge was big, but rather than rising to it, I started to fear it. I allowed my great expectations to erode. I yielded to a self-proclaimed, fear-based future.

Then something happened that really changed my perspective. A friend came to town to see the church. He pulled into the driveway, and I showed him the church building. The auditorium was old but rather large, about six hundred seats. Then I walked around the neighborhood and showed him a few houses that the church owned. His reaction to what he saw was nothing like mine. He said, "This place is incredible!" He went on to tell me about how much possibility was in this church and what could be done. He glowed with spectacular faith and began to prophesy a future to a preacher who had no hope. He saw what I did not see. He went on and on about the neighborhood being transformed and the "foundations being restored." He did not rebuke my negative attitude. He did something better: He stepped on my toes in a beautiful kind of way. He changed the scenery for me. Before that, all I could see was lack and devastation. My friend saw an opportunity and a future.

We need people in our lives like him, people who will not sympathize with our plight but who instead will show us the opportunity around us. In a way this is a form of rebuke, but the person does not get into your face. Instead, he speaks encouragement regarding your impossible situation. Without downplaying your struggle, he provides a fresh set of eyes on the problem. This is nothing like a sit-down conversation in which someone tells you things about your life that need to change. These are just observations about the good all around that you may not have seen in a long time.

That day changed my life. I decided I was going to start seeing everything as an asset rather than a liability. Instead of trying to hide the fact that we had an old building in a tough community, I started to speak like my friend. From that point on, I started to say things like, "Come back to the heart of the city, and let's build something great together!" We did not have a church building with an elegant lobby or magnificent children's play spaces as many megachurches do, but we had a compelling mission to feed the poor, house the homeless and use every square inch of our building to serve the broken.

A strange thing happened—that message began to resonate. The very thing I thought was a barrier to reaching the city became the drawing card to bring people back into the city. People were driving from the suburbs back into Los Angeles because they wanted to be a part of restoring the city. Families in fancy cars showed up and said, "Pastor, we're with you for life, and we want to raise our kids around hurting people." They said, "We don't need to be catered to. We want the legacy of our family to be serving others. We want to disciple our kids in missions through the heartbeat of this church." I warned parents that the kids we would bring to church would cuss and have no background of faith, and the people who were being drawn here loved that aspect. (I mean, they did not like the cussing, but they loved the reality that a messy church is a beautiful church.)

> Decide to be a provoker of greatness. Show people the beauty of their lives and keep them from being dulled by their daily routine.

This radical change happened through one man who stepped on my toes and showed me that what I had was so much more incredible than what I thought I lacked.

Decide to be a provoker of greatness. Step on toes! Break into your friend's pity party and point out the good that exists even when his world seems to be collapsing around him. Show people the beauty of their lives and keep them from being dulled by their daily routine.

The Bible says, "Open rebuke is better than secret love" (Proverbs 27:5 KJV). Rebuke comes in different forms, and this is the best one I have found. The most powerful rebukes in my life came when someone simply shined more brightly than I could in my circumstances, reminding me with childlike faith in their eyes of the joy that I was missing.

MY SMALL STEP 6

After reading about this step and taking some time to pray, write down the small step you will take to follow God's nudge.

STEP 7

Step Out of Yourself

"What's in it for me?"—the phrase of our generation. The "you benefit" craze is everywhere in the media, books, conferences. Everyone is on a journey to find happiness. We even strategize about how we can interact with people to change them to be the way we want them to be. We want a world that fits into our mold of happiness. We are on a senseless treadmill, trying to make the world conform to what we think we want.

In my experience, we rarely know what we really want or need, so why do we keep trying? Could the answer be in getting as far away from ourselves as possible? And by that I mean starving ourselves of all the things we think we need to make ourselves happy and just deciding to live outside of ourselves. Rather than craving praise, give it freely to others. Instead of seeking to be appreciated, become the one who appreciates.

It is difficult to stop thinking, *I need certain things to make me happy. The world must conform to my five-year plan, or I will not have joy.* Maybe the script needs to be thrown out. What new worlds await when we step out of ourselves and stop obsessing about what we think will make *us* happy and instead begin to serve others? The script that tells us what will make us happy is usually a false narrative.

Step into Joy

People write to me about how spending a year volunteering at the Dream Center was the hardest year of their lives financially but the greatest year in every other way. I have found that nothing has ever gone according to my plan in building this church. Everything is changing all the time. I cannot let the highs and lows determine my value or calculate my joy.

The darkest place I have ever lived is in the place of comparison, worrying about where I am versus where I want to be. It is a trap, quicksand, death. That is not the life God has for us. Lamentations 3:22–23 (ESV) declares, "The steadfast love of the LORD never ceases; his mercies never come to an end; they are new every morning; great is your faithfulness." We need to cultivate a life of prayerfulness in order to remember that truth.

Prayer breaks life down into the simplest of terms. It reminds us of what really matters and that we have a new start every day. In the presence of God the small, hidden things in our lives get exposed, and when we deal with them we find freedom. I have never come out of a time of prayer holding a grudge or wanting to chew someone out. Prayer resets our priorities and gets us focused on the things that will carry us to the finish line.

Life is full of small steps, and we usually view them as the bridge that gets us somewhere bigger and better. But could it be that the small steps have the biggest impact of all? We have all heard stories of people who accomplished something great only to go into a deep depression afterward. Once I spoke to an athlete who won a Super Bowl and the very next week wanted to take his own life. A businessman can close a big deal yet fail to close a void in his heart. Could it be that we are missing something? Could the small things in life actually bring us the most joy?

God made us for victory every day, and those daily victories have nothing to do with profits, fame or acclaim. The path to true joy lies in deciding to live outside of ourselves and to be intentional about breaking the biggest barrier to our

> I have never come out of a time of prayer holding a grudge or wanting to chew someone out. Prayer resets our priorities and gets us focused on the things that will carry us to the finish line.

joy—our own selfishness. Living outside of ourselves means living in rebellion to the constant feeding of our flesh, which demands to be recognized, appreciated and respected. Living outside of ourselves means deciding to serve and give instead of waiting to be served.

Try it! Test the waters and see if you find more value in living this way.

Step Out of Selfishness

If I had the power to fight in only one area of my life, throwing all my energy into opposing one particular weakness, I would oppose selfishness. I firmly believe that all of the dominos will fall once we decide to take on that horrible monster.

Once I was watching a Northern California high school track meet online. It was an 800-meter race, which is two laps around the track. The gun went off, and the girl in the lead took off. She ran a 59-second first lap, which is extremely fast, and she was in the lead all the way up to the 700-meter mark. It appeared that she was going to win in a mind-boggling record time. (The winner of this race would qualify for the CIF California State Meet, the pinnacle of the track and field season.) Suddenly, her legs gave out and she collapsed. Her body had shut down because of a virus from the night before.

The girl in second place shockingly found herself in first. She passed the fallen girl, and then she did something amazing. She stopped and took a few steps back to help the girl get back to her feet. Now, this was her rival, her biggest obstacle to winning the state title. Yet she went back and not only helped her up by lending her hand, but also yelled at her, "Get up and qualify!" And they both got to the finish line in time to qualify for the state level. To that runner, the value of reaching out in service outweighed the very real possibility of coming in first, well ahead of her greatest competitor. That is living outside of yourself!

None of the people who knew that young woman best were surprised by her courageous act. She valued service and selflessness; they came out of the overflow of who she was as a person.

I believe that when you become intentional about living outside of yourself, you will start to live a life of service instinctively. Soon you will find more joy in doing good daily than in achieving your big dreams. Society teaches you to value accomplishment, but God wants you to see victory in who you are becoming. By defeating selfishness, you are accomplishing something great, and you can have this victory every day of your life.

> When you become intentional about living outside of yourself, you will start to live a life of service instinctively.

Have you ever gone to a function where a high-level executive or well-respected person in ministry is conducting a question-and-answer session? People usually ask about the secret behind their rise to the top. I have observed that older people do not ask that question. They seem more concerned about the character of the person than about their accomplishments. Life has taught them that choosing to live outside of yourself is truly the happiest place to be, not competing against others, but rather helping others achieve their best. This is the ultimate high point of success.

> Jesus was the ultimate example of self-sacrifice, and in His 33 years of walking this earth, He showed us that the only true way to live is to empty yourself.

A selfish life is a prison. It violates the very Word of God because it is such a complete contrast to the Savior who gave His life on the cross. Our heavenly Father relinquished His precious, beloved Son: "For God so loved the world that he gave his one and only Son, that whoever believes in him shall not perish but have eternal life" (John 3:16). Jesus was the ultimate example of self-sacrifice, and in His 33 years of walking this earth, He showed us that the only true way to live is to empty yourself.

Bypass Your Failures

Have you ever had a spontaneous idea as a parent to go off and do something fun with your kids? One day we were sitting at home on a Friday night and I told the kids, "Let's go to Disneyland," which of course is not very far away from us. I was just following the nudge. The kids were so excited, jumping up and down.

Within fifteen minutes, we were in the car heading down the free-way. It was perfect. I pumped up the radio, and we were cruising. Suddenly we hit traffic, and I mean bad traffic. Los Angeles traffic is the worst. Whenever I face it, I have learned to pause, collect myself and tell myself to breathe. This tactic usually works for about half an hour.

This day, that was not long enough. I snapped. I just went on a rant. I threw my hands up in the air, and I screamed at other cars. I pounded the steering wheel in full-on toddler mode. My kids were looking at me as if someone had kidnapped their real dad. We finally arrived at Disneyland, and of course the parking structure where we had to park was full, and cars were backed up almost fifteen minutes just to pay to get in. Eventually we parked the car and started walking toward the park, only to encounter another line for checking people's bags. I proceeded to lose it again, raging to my kids, "Why are these people bringing so many bags into this park?"

Then I stopped and looked at my kids, whose faces had been so happy an hour before. Now they looked so sad. My selfish response had killed the moment and taken all the fun away from my generous idea. Now I had become the Grinch. It is amazing how quickly one initial selfish act can grow into a wrecking ball of destruction. Taking offense at traffic had reduced me to a frantic menace.

However, it is not impossible to pivot and change direction, deciding to take one small step toward the good even when we have wandered. I turned to my kids and said these exact words: "I'm sorry for being so angry. From this moment until midnight, I'm going to be the happiest dad you've ever seen." A simple shift in my head occurred, and I followed through with it. This was not a huge epiphany, but it was a nudge from the Holy Spirit. From that point on, we ran from ride to ride and ate everything we wanted, experiencing everything. We went hard for the next six hours. It turned out to be the best experience we have ever had at Disneyland. A negative experience got transformed into a positive one because I had let goodness prevail over the selfishness in my soul.

With God's help, we can step out of selfishness at any time. A life of selfishness is a defensive life, a life of self-preservation. A life of generosity is a life on offensive attack. As *The Message* puts it, "The world of the generous gets larger and larger; the world of the stingy gets smaller and smaller" (Proverbs 11:24).

Decide to Step Free

This is one of the reasons serving other people is such a major part of our recovery program at the Dream Center. The world of someone who has been controlled for a long time by alcohol or drugs is a selfish world. *How can I feel better? How can I obtain whatever will get me high?*

In our one-year program we try to supplant that mindset by inviting people to start taking steps toward freedom by thinking about others. A big part of the program entails going out into the streets, cleaning the neighborhood and serving within the program. We know that the best version of ourselves is the one that is lived outward. We thrive in a life of service.

Generosity sets us free, like opening a cage sets a bird free. Generosity is not just about money; it is a way of seeing life. We give ourselves the permission to say good things we were afraid to say. We decide to do good things such as going to visit parents who might not have been good to us when we were children, loving them simply because it is the right thing to do. It might be hard, but it is worth it. We accept

> Generosity sets us free, like opening a cage sets a bird free.

the cost of the effort because we know that anything noble will cost something.

This kind of generosity can be applied to a marriage in which both parties feel offended and each has a case. After years and years of living in a stalemate over who will crack first, the generous one simply says, "I'm sorry," and healing starts to occur. You have heard the old saying, "It takes two to tango." But it takes only one to abandon selfishness and make peace.

I love the movie *The Grinch*. What I love the most about the movie is the symbolism of this wounded soul who decided to live on a hill in a pile of trash. He became comfortable with his identity in the hurt of his past. His reward for his bitterness was sitting on a pile of rubbish. His heart became smaller as his offenses grew in intensity. At the end of the movie, he hears the villagers singing Christmas songs, and he is overcome with love, which makes his heart become larger and larger. He opened himself to a new world.

Good things happen when we step away from the garbage of life and open our hearts, when we feel the Holy Spirit calling us away from whatever is holding us back.

Take the First Step

Every one of us can take baby steps and turn to follow Him. Try it out—try serving out of your pain rather than identifying with it. Experiment, test the waters, see if you like life much better without resentment or grudges. Take that first one small step away from yourself and just see what happens.

I constantly remind our staff and residents at the Dream Center to get used to saying yes more often than no. I have found that it is so much easier to try to do something than to explain why it cannot be done. We cannot always calculate and rationalize everything in life. We must instinctively live it and figure it out along the way.

A man has been coming to our church for over two decades. He rides the church bus for every service, and it is incredible that he has been coming to the same church for so long. Every service he comes up to me and says, "I like your shoes!" This precious man is dealing with mental disabilities. One day I said, "Next week I'm going to give you some new shoes." He was so happy and excited to get his new shoes.

The only problem was I needed some size 14 shoes. About fifteen minutes later, I was standing at the back door of the church, and a man who trains NBA pros said, "I've got a pair of size 14 shoes if anyone needs them." I looked up at God and smiled at the familiar provision of heaven that occurs when we choose to act in faith. I said, "I'll take them." The next week before church, he brought a whole bag of brand-new size 14 shoes. I walked up to the man and said, "I got you some shoes!" He made a squeaky sound of joy when he saw the sack full of size 14 basketball shoes, and he looked like a little child opening his Christmas gifts.

This really was not a heroic deed at all, but then something else happened. Another man was sitting nearby, watching all this unfold five minutes before the service. He had just started to go to church again and was curious about faith. This one simple deed touched his heart profoundly. He came to me later and said, "Seeing you give that man those shoes inspired me to give my life to Christ." I was thrilled to hear the news, but I could hardly believe that this man would give his life to Christ simply because he witnessed one good deed. He later went on to explain that he had not seen anything good in a long time and something about that experience drew him to want to know the goodness of Christ.

We live in such a selfish, cutthroat world. That means that any good deed stands out, and it really can spark an interest in faith. As John wrote, "The light shines in the darkness, and the darkness has not overcome it" (John 1:5). My new understanding of this verse is that one good deed can overwhelm years and years of darkness. The world seems to be more and more astonished by ordinary acts of kindness. I have noticed that simple things carry more weight than ever before. The rush of life to accomplish more, be more, do more has stirred people into such a frantic pace that when anyone stops to do something kind, it takes them by surprise.

> We live in such a selfish, cutthroat world. That means that any good deed stands out, and it really can spark an interest in faith.

Even giving a cold cup of water in His name holds tremendous value. Or switching seats on an airplane. Have you ever been on an airplane where a couple has been split up and wants to exchange seats with another passenger so they can sit together? Sometimes it turns into quite an ordeal if too many people refuse to give up their precious seat. Is the reward of having your particular seat greater than the reward of making someone else happy? No, but temporary convenience and the prevailing need for self-preservation seem to win too often.

People always ask how is it that I have been able to stay at the same church in a tough neighborhood for 25 years. More times than I can count, this ministry should have died from lack of funds, inability to make fire code requirements and the constant need for last-minute miracles. The secret has truly been to learn how to live outside of myself. If I internalize everything, my world will collapse to a perspective based on my struggles and my limited view of what is going on. If I view only the bad things, I will shrink to match the environment around me. However, if I choose to give something away (especially something that I would rather keep), it makes my world bigger. I remember my call, and I find joy in being available and used by God.

Make the Most of the Moment

No better possession or place or higher accomplishment will ever make us happy. This is the great lie of the enemy: *When I get _____, then I'll be happy.* We are already here, in the moment. Make the most of it by finding a way to make a difference in the daily routines of life.

You will be remembered by the traits of your character far more than by anything you may accomplish. People say to me all the time, "Pastor, if I don't feel something, I'm not going to fake it."

My response: "You need to fake it even if you don't feel it. That's called character." Character is choosing to give someone something they need even though you need it, too. This is not avoiding being true to yourself—it is the purest form of love. You need something, you are tired, you have nothing to give, but you still give away kindness because something in you has the character to push beyond feelings and find a way to bless.

In sports when a player pushes his boundaries late in the game, the commentators say, "He found that extra something." We all have that something in us that we can give even when we would rather hide in the corner of our heart and wait for something good to come our way. We can *make* good things happen by daring to step out of ourselves and venture out into the world of serving others, even when we need to be served ourselves.

Every Thursday night at church we have a guest speaker at the Dream Center. This is remarkable because right in the middle of downtown Los Angeles two thousand people gather together, braving traffic to get to church. I marvel that week after week, year after year, people find a way to get through the gridlock to attend church. The speakers who come to visit the Dream Center are friends of the ministry, and our weekly revival meeting has become a shining light in the city.

People laugh at me because even after all these years, when the speaker gets up, I still do this quirky thing: I sit at the very edge of my seat to listen to the sermon. I mean so far off the edge that if I moved one more inch, I would fall off the seat. In fact, a few times I have actually fallen off my seat listening to a sermon. People take my picture, and it is quite hilarious how I can avoid a wipeout while almost dangling off the seat. Why do I do this? Because years ago when I was a teenage evangelist, I would travel to churches to speak and I would notice that often the pastors were not interested in what I had to say. Many of them (not all) would fold their arms and look around or get up to check on something in another room while church was going on. After years of that, I made a pledge to myself as a young man that one day when I had my own church, I would become the biggest cheerleader and best listener for every guest pastor who came to my church to speak. I made a personal vow that no matter how tired I was or what I was going through, I would serve that pastor by becoming an encourager in the front row.

Admittedly, I can go over the top shouting and fist-pumping, and sometimes my wife will have to elbow me. But that does not change the simple truth: Make the effort to get outside of yourself and put yourself in another's world. God has given us the ability to create. We are His creations and therefore we, too, have creative power. We can transform our daily experiences by adopting the right attitude that refuses to be stuck in a self-absorbed world.

Parents, keep encouraging your teenage kids all the time. Even if you feel they are not getting what you say, keep saying it, because you *are* reaching them. Whatever you do for others will not always show up on the surface, but it has an impact—and it changes *you* along the way. Almost for sure, the words you speak are getting through, but even if they are not, you yourself are becoming something beautiful, sustainable and useful for the Kingdom of God. A life of encouragement has a resounding effect for years to come.

Small Tweets of Kindness

Sometimes I will send something out on social media that I feel in my heart will bless someone. One day I felt led to send out a tweet to encourage people who might be dealing with slow progress. This is the message I posted on Twitter: "Having too much too soon doesn't usually end up too well. The slow build teaches us to celebrate small gains, which is necessary to stay the course."

Funny thing—I sent that out, and it met with little response. It was kind of a dud. Yet the days went on, and people began to like it and retweet it. Weeks went by, months went by, and that little tweet still lingered in the Twitter universe. Thousands were passing it around. When the tweet was sent out, it met with no response. But encouragement lingers and eventually it makes its impact.

Small steps of kindness and encouragement matter. They may float around for a while, but then at the right time they will become a blessing to someone. Even today, people are still liking that tweet and sending it out, and some are even framing it for their offices.

It shows how a lot of encouragement—or even just saying some little thing you think will help someone—usually takes a little time to resonate and find a landing spot. The words you say to your kids on the way home from school might not seem to hit home today, but one day in the midst of college pressures and temptation and struggle, those kind words will float up from their souls and set up little tents of refuge.

> The legacy of a servant lives on, and the nature of a giver never dies.

When we live outside ourselves, the little memories we create for others provide daily reminders that our life is so much bigger than our trials, struggles or limitations. When we choose to stop internalizing every experience and step outside ourselves, we add life to our years. The legacy of a servant lives on, and the nature of a giver never dies.

Lose Yourself

A popular expression in our culture is the phrase "Find yourself." Interestingly, the Word of God tells us that the opposite is true: "Whoever finds their life will lose it, and whoever loses their life for my sake will find it" (Matthew 10:39).

The best way to illustrate losing yourself and living outside of yourself is to introduce you to two people who live at the Dream Center. Their names are Craig and Sandra Kinart. For years they attended my father's church in Phoenix, Arizona. During the aftermath of Hurricane Katrina in 2005, they decided to take a mission trip to the Dream Center, where we were housing hurricane evacuees from Louisiana. The need was so great that evacuees were being flown from Baton Rouge to Los Angeles to be housed at the Dream Center.

This was by far one of the most trying times in Dream Center history. Every day people would get off a plane at a private jet runway in Burbank that had been offered by a wealthy man for the use of evacuee relocation, and each of them had nothing left but a few belongings in a plastic bag. The moment they stepped off the plane, news reporters shoved microphones into their faces, asking them to talk about their experiences and following them to the Dream Center. The normal routines of the Dream Center were turned upside down in 24 hours. We had no plan in place for such an emergency, so we just had to respond and figure it out later. Twice a day, evacuees were flooding into our building, and people's lives were in shambles.

Even Dr. Phil showed up and did a show about trauma, which was good—except that we were trying to settle people down and the presence of the media hindered our ability to help people get through the day. We had no clue how to feed more people or how to create a long-term transition plan for them in addition to housing our current residents. Media trucks camped outside our building around the clock.

Honestly, it drove me close to quitting the ministry because I could not see a way out of this massive responsibility. Then, once again, God showed up. When God shows up it is usually in the form of people who can bring you out of the way you feel. If you feel lifeless, God sends you people with life. If you are hopeless, He will send you people of contagious hope. Craig and Sandy showed up at our greatest hour of need—and they saw the situation as a blessing.

What gripped their hearts the most was the men's and women's recovery program. They understood that we needed to keep our existing programs strong during the hurricane relief work, so they just threw themselves into volunteering in the recovery program. Their mission trip turned into a stay that was a lot longer than the single week they had intended. A month later they were still serving, and they had become the glue that kept the program together during the chaos. Gripped by their experience, they decided to stay at the Dream Center and have now been here for over fourteen years.

When I heard about this plan, I tried to stop it. I did not want them to lose everything they had to come here. Sell everything? Move into a hospital room at the Dream Center? Live on the same floor as all the men coming off the street? I did not want them to sacrifice so much. (Why do we put up barriers when people simply want to do good? We cannot know what is in their hearts, and we tend to underestimate them.)

They came and moved in with former prisoners as their neighbors on the same hospital floor. Years later, they are still on that floor, still working for free. I offered them some money so they could move off the floor into an apartment to get away from the day-to-day grind of ministry. They have turned down that offer repeatedly for over a decade. Their retirement package has included the payment of seeing former addicts, prisoners and twenty-year drug-users walking across the stage at church, receiving their graduation diplomas. They are the happiest people I know, the most consistent, the most stable.

In my 25 years of pastoring the same church, every person I have met that has consistent character and demonstrates noticeable attributes of being a follower of Christ has always been someone who freely lives outside of him- or herself. They do not overthink life. They do not internalize everything in terms of how it pertains to their personal feelings. Instead, they just live in the beautiful place of being aware of other people and their needs. They find joy in living outside of themselves.

MY SMALL STEP 7

After reading about this step and taking some time to pray, write down the small step you will take to follow God's nudge.

STEP 8

When You Feel
You Cannot Move

So far this book has been about taking steps—big steps and small steps—stepping out of comfort zones and deciding to make the effort to move forward boldly and courageously. This presupposes that you can put one foot in front of the other and take those steps. Therefore, the question that needs to be asked is, What do you do when you cannot move?

You might be in a season of your life right now where you simply have nothing left to give, and you feel paralyzed. One of the greatest men of action in the Bible felt this way. King David was a man of courage, full of faith and prepared to step toward any challenge. As a boy he had been willing to take on a giant, and as a man he was always ready to go to battle with his troops. King David was even secure and confident enough to celebrate the return of the Ark of the Covenant by stripping down and dancing in an undignified way in the midst of the common people of the land. He was a mover and shaker, a man who was willing to fly high and live boldly. His motto could have been "Go big or go home."

However, even the greats come to a place where their lives come to a crashing halt. In Psalm 32, we find a different David. Here is a man who was overwhelmed by his sinful actions, a man whose bones were wasting away (see verse 3). He had lost his energy: "My strength was sapped as in the heat of summer" (verse 4). This is not the same David who had taunted Goliath by telling him he was about to feed his body to the birds (see 1 Samuel 17:44). What had happened to him?

Heroes get tired. Faithful people run up against walls and run out of gas. Life wears us down. Unrelenting schedules grow uninspiring. Facing life's battles and struggles can leave you feeling as if a heavyweight boxer is leaning on you day after day while you are immobilized, pressed up against the ropes, just hoping to be saved by the bell.

I think Psalm 32 is one of my favorite chapters in the Bible because it feels like real life. One of God's greatest generals of all time is expressing his desire to throw in the towel. Dying on the inside, he has nothing left to give, nor does he sound too motivated to get it back. This is an all-too-familiar place in life—shutting down, just existing, letting time take its gradual course, fading into the sunset.

In Psalm 32, David is working through some issues, and he is permitting us to have a front-row seat as he does so. Beautifully, he comes back to a wonderful resting place: confession and worship. He realizes that he does not have to win any battles, and he does not have to perform; he just needs to take some time to get back to his roots of worshiping and being with God. The tone of the psalm starts to change as David reminds himself that when he has recovered his relationship with God, he has everything.

Rest in Him

What do you do when you can no longer move, when stagnation takes over? Nothing! As a child of God, you sink back to your roots. Who are you and what were you made to do? Worship.

Think of it this way: In the *Rocky* movies, every time Rocky loses a battle he always goes back to the roots of his training. He will leave the fancy gym and either run up the Russian mountains, go to an old gym with no air conditioning or (in the latest movie) take the boxer he is training to the desert. Whenever he loses, he always knows where to get his edge back.

How do we get our fighter's edge back? By returning to the fundamentals of our faith, which include prayer and worship. David found his "Rocky moment" by opening his life up to God once again. He went back to the vulnerability of the basics. The enemy tries to steal our courage by creating long periods of separation from the presence of God. He knows that he has reason to be afraid if our next move is the powerful one of refocusing on Christ.

I must admit that I have learned this the hard way. There was a season of my life in ministry when I felt lifeless. For the whole 25 years I have been a pastor, I stand every week at the back door to shake people's hands after church. I have loved that part of ministry— meeting new people and just loving on them. Yet for a time it seemed that almost every week somebody would try to corner me for a meeting or somebody needed me to take care of something that was meant for another day. Sometimes people were trying to hustle their way to the top of the housing list at the Dream Center by going through me rather than the proper channels.

Honestly, I got sick of people. I felt used and underappreciated, and I know I was just plain tired and selfish. I was doing my job because

I knew how to do it, but my heart was not in it. I loved people from a distance, but I was drifting from them up close and personal. It got to the point where I would come into worship during the second song and leave right out the back door after church. This phase went on for over a year. I still loved people; I was just tired of being used. When I would walk into a room full of people and their demands, I felt as though a piece of me was being picked away with every demand. I was also overwhelmed by the very nature of our ministry, which involves surviving financially week after week after week. I was so sick of walking the tightrope every week. I just wanted to get away from people.

One day I went into God's presence with nothing to give but whining and complaints. My spirit was so "off." I even told God that I had a cold and rebellious heart, and I begged Him to rebuke and correct me.

How grateful I am that God does not always answer our prayers in the way we think He should. He did not give me the lashing that I thought I deserved. Instead, He spoke words of encouragement to me. He reminded me of how good people had been to me all the years. I replayed the scenarios in my mind of all the times miracles showed up on the doorstep of the Dream Center, when people wanted to give us an offering or help in a practical way to keep us going. He showed me the church members who put up with me when I was not at my best. He reminded me of the goodness of humanity, and then He gently reminded me to start loving people the way He had loved me when I was needy and selfish. I dusted myself off and decided that feeling underappreciated or used was never really the issue—it was my heart disconnected from the presence of God for long periods of time.

I love how God allows us to work through our difficulties in His presence. With most other people, we can never be as vulnerable as we can be with God. We can go to God with a puzzle of missing pieces and have no idea how to put it together again, and God will carefully help us put it back together. You can throw the kitchen sink at God, and it does not bother Him, because He is just so happy that you are back in fellowship again.

I did not need advice. I just needed to tell God everything I was going through. I knew He would never judge me. So many times I have talked about my pain to God, and I have been healed simply by venting. At the end of such a complaint session, I have felt God's love and that was enough. I did not need a word of advice or correction.

What do you do when you cannot move? Just decide to rest. As the psalmist says, "Be still, and know that I am God" (Psalm 46:10).

> "Be still, and know that I am God."

Fortified for the Future

Before any great advance, you will usually experience a time of simply staying put and letting His strength return. He will make sure that you are ready for the next surge of life ahead.

Once the very vigorous Elijah was shut down completely (see 1 Kings 19). Elijah had no problem going up against the hundreds of prophets of Baal, nor was he afraid of the king's wrath. What shut him down was the queen, Jezebel. She vowed to take his life, and he ran away. He fled even though hers was a much more inferior challenge than what he faced with the prophets of Baal.

In a similar way, we, too, can rise to the occasion in big challenges of our lives, only to wilt under a far lesser attack. Yet God did not rebuke Elijah for being overly fearful, nor did He question his faith or his courage. God did not condemn him for his desire to die, nor did He call him out for being cowardly after being so bold.

God's remedy was to send him shelter and sleep. A lot of sleep! God knew that this man had been on the move, stepping up to incredible challenges. An angel woke him up to give him food, and it was not just ordinary food. God knew he needed supernatural empowerment to get back up and walk for forty days and nights. He would need to fire on all cylinders, but first he had to regain his mental strength, to clear the slate of his mind from those past experiences and to renew his purpose.

Worship and rest go hand in hand. Our lives will sometimes come to a screeching halt, and that is for a good reason—because God needs us to stop and regain the strength we will need for the next place He is taking us. The most courageous thing we can do may not be to keep moving when we are tired but rather to receive true rest so that we can undertake the next step.

Worship and rest go hand in hand.

In those Elijah moments, God puts you into a season of rest, and you come out on the other side so much better. Clarity of mind returns. No longer are you forcing what you do with so much effort; you are able to do things with a clarity of direction. No longer does your significance come from moving so fast. Resting allows you to understand that more can happen with one clear thought that comes from being in God's presence than with banging your head against the wall trying to churn out more effort.

In the case of Elijah, God knew that Elijah had struggled and fought as much as he possibly could. Now he needed a break, a time when he could be loved back to life. There are surges to momentum in all our callings. Sometimes things just seem to work even when we do less, and sometimes, no matter how hard we work, we struggle to succeed. What season are you in right now? Maybe God is calling you to shelter, and He wants to feed you for the next push ahead. Maybe the next step you need to take is not outward but inward—to receive His invitation of refuge. There is no five-star resort in the world that can do more for your walk with God than your prayer closet can.

Never Enough but Always Enough

I remember the day so clearly—June 5, 2019, the day when the Los Angeles homeless population statistics were released. We knew the numbers were rising, but we were all stunned by the report from the Los Angeles Homeless Service Authority that homelessness had increased twelve percent in one year. That puts the count at 58,936, which is more people than would fill up Dodger Stadium. The return to downtown Los Angeles of diseases like the bubonic plague was being discussed as a very real possibility in the future.

Then there is the mental health component. One of the main contributing factors to homelessness is untreated mental health issues. Often when I give tours of the Dream Center, people ask me, "What do you guys do about people who are facing mental challenges?" My answer always startles people because many believe we should turn them away.

My answer? "We take them in." There are cases that might require something that we do not provide, but the truth is that people can change. Rather than giving up on people who are mentally ill and serving them by putting public toilets in homeless encampments, we believe people can be healed and rehabilitated. We have seen it happen. When people come into our program for a year, they have the luxury of time to change. A thirty-day program is not long enough to deal with years and years of root issues (and truthfully, even our one-year program does not feel long enough). Yet one year in God's presence, one year under the shelter of worship, one year of being with a community of believers—that has more power than any drug. We have pledged not to be terrified by the term *mental illness*, but instead to welcome people into our family to experience the healing power of God's Word and to receive restoration in His presence.

This fits with what I was saying about rest. I believe that sometimes it takes more discipline to rest than it does to keep striving and running on empty. Progress is found in resting, and the best gift we can give our family and the world is a renewed heart and rejuvenated purpose.

When you feel that you cannot move anymore, do what David and Elijah did: Go (frequently, if you can) into a quiet place where you do not have to perform and where you can receive encouragement and even a new assignment for what is next. When everything seems impossible and stagnation feels endless, realize that *enduring* is the bridge that gets you where you need to go.

When our family took a trip to see the Grand Canyon, we knew we would be seeing one of the seven natural wonders of the world, but the drive was long. We were excited about getting there, but we had to endure a long car trip that was very uninspiring. We drove for miles and miles through an endless landscape of dirt and weeds, hearing only the impatient sounds of kids saying, "Are we almost there?" Similarly, the drive to achieve something great entails days, weeks, months and even sometimes decades when nothing but dirt and tumbleweeds seem to make up the scenery. We need to realize that those long stretches are not meaningless. As a matter of fact, they are the key to get you where you need to go.

> Sometimes it takes more discipline to rest than it does to keep striving and running on empty.

Sudden success can be very dangerous. I know many young pastors who have had breakout beginnings in ministry, and the speed of success takes them where they never thought they could be. Social media has a way of drawing people in, and overnight successes do occur. A carefully crafted image can take you somewhere quickly, but only character and depth will get you to the finish line. If sudden success transpires, praise God for it. But immediately run to the soil of your heart to make sure your spiritual foundations will be able to outpace your accomplishments.

When we started the Dream Center, there was a lot of buzz about my father coming to Los Angeles to take over a church that needed revival. The old Bethel Temple where we started was one of the first Assembly of God churches planted out of the Azusa Street Revival in 1906. The news spread that my father, Tommy Barnett, would attempt to rebuild that historic church, which was located in a gang-infested community. The first week we showed up, the building was packed. We were greeted with arms wide open. Eight hundred people filled the building, all of them curious about this new venture. The atmosphere was electric with emerging new hope. There was only one problem—my well-known dad was just planting the church, not staying. He was not coming back the following week. He had his own church to pastor in Phoenix. I was going to be the pastor, and I was not my dad. The next week our attendance dropped from eight hundred to around twenty. It was terrifying. This would be the true test of character. There were now more people at any given time in the restrooms of my father's church than in my entire congregation!

Fast-forward to today. In my best-case scenario, I could never have orchestrated what God has done, providing a landmark hospital and many outreaches, with Dream Centers spreading all over the world.

There were times when success was defined as merely surviving the day or simply waking up and deciding to pray. The valley on the way to success was very long, but God gave us the season of nothingness so that what we built would last. Today the Dream Center is one of the only institutions in our community that still exists decades after its founding.

Sheltered

That long season of no progress caused me to do something very important, and that was to learn to pray and think. I thank God all the time for lack of momentum in the early days, because if God had given me early success in the traditional sense of building a church, I would never have taken the prayer walks necessary to see the need in my community, which instigated a church model built on 24-hour service to the surrounding community.

The idea of the Dream Center was not born out of a season of success; it was born into a season when God sheltered me and showed me what it was like to feel loved. His shelter gave me a vision to shelter others the same way He had sheltered me. The early failures were the best things that could have happened to me because they forced me to seek God, and I came away feeling validated and loved by Him. I needed to feel God's love because He wanted me to be able to give it away one day. When we feel loved, we start dreaming crazy dreams because we are dreaming through God's heart.

The idea of the Dream Center came from a season of prayer walks and rest. Having a church that was open 24/7 was not part of my original ambition. The vision came to me when I was resting in a relationship with God. I tell young pastors all the time: *Commit yourself not to success but to faithfulness, and everything will take care of itself.*

Learn to love every part of your calling, even when it means simply showing up with nothing dynamic happening along the way. Remember that we must go through the boring scenery to get to the majestic views of life. When we get there, we will see that it was worth it. What seems to be going backward is going forward if you look at the journey this way. If you are succeeding, of course that is fun; we all love to see tangible signs of success. But even if you reach a plateau, that is fine as well. Look at it as a base camp on a climb up Mount Everest and enjoy residing at that altitude to acclimate to the next push up the mountain.

I am sure David felt that he had lost all the momentum of his career after his impossible victory over Goliath. Nothing seemed to come of his victory, and recognition was replaced by lonely nights and self-doubt. After the soaring high point, he was a nobody. His only crime? Being brave enough to do what others would not do. To the people, David was a one-hit wonder, and his fifteen minutes of fame for killing Goliath was the high point of his career. But God was up to something behind the scenes, something greater than Goliath hitting the canvas in a knockout victory; He was building the character of a man who was only in the early days of his career. David needed to be ready for something beyond his wildest dreams.

> We must go through the boring scenery to get to the majestic views of life. When we get there, we will see that it was worth it.

Then he had to spend some time hiding in the cave of Adullam right after the biggest victory of his life (see 1 Samuel 22:1–2). The principle is the same for us; the best days of our lives are usually spent in caves and seasons of self-doubt, and when we choose to embrace those seasons, God can build us to last, which is His goal for our lives. The enemy has a terrible habit of underestimating what God can do with a surrendered soul who feels stuck.

Underestimated?

I think one of the reasons the Word of God touches our lives so deeply is because in it we can read about the many people who experienced the ebbs and flows of momentum. Through all of the highs and lows, ups and downs, God is always there, displaying His heart (and His glory) for those who are underestimated by the world around them. The world praises people who are at the peak of their performance, strength and power, those who can do great things. Our God looks for the people who have been cast aside, who might feel like a shadow of their former selves, who feel stuck. He has a special love for the tired, the overlooked, the underestimated. If you feel underestimated, overwhelmed and intimidated, then with His help, you are qualified to change the world.

A wonderful, elderly lady who is on the board of the Dream Center told me something one day when I was going through a very difficult season in my life and everything felt as if it was collapsing. She looked me in the eye and with a stern face and pointy finger said these words: "Never let anyone take away your face of peace." She went on to say, "As long as you keep waiting on the Lord, you will never lose your face of peace." The face of peace reflects a life that is usable, redeemable, teachable and ready.

I love what Robert Schuller once said: "Tough times don't last. Tough people do." Give God your heart in the middle of your brokenness because the best version of you is not the one you thought was the best version; the best version of you is the one God is about to create. When you present the shattered pieces of your life to God, He is not scared off or overwhelmed. If while driving down the road, you or I see the shattered pieces of something, we do what we can to get out of the way. When God sees the shattered pieces of someone's life, He does not go around them. Instead, He picks them up and puts them back together again. Just when you think everything is over, God comes down and does something incredible to let you know it has just begun.

Our hope is expressed so well in these verses:

We also glory in our sufferings, because we know that suffering produces perseverance; perseverance, character; and character, hope. And hope does not put us to shame, because God's love has been poured out into our hearts through the Holy Spirit, who has been given to us.

Romans 5:3–5

MY SMALL STEP 8

After reading about this step and taking some time to pray, write down the small step you will take to follow God's nudge.

STEP 9

One Small Thought

When I was a young man, I remember driving with my father on his weekly trip to his favorite frozen yogurt place. He loved this little place right down the street from our house. Honestly, I do not really like yogurt; I prefer ice cream. But it gave my dad pure joy, so I went along for the ride. Like clockwork every Tuesday at seven o'clock, we would park the car, eat our frozen yogurt outside in the setting Arizona sun, and just talk about life, ministry or anything.

My father is such an enjoyable person to be around. One of the reasons I love to spend time with him is because he is one of the only men I have ever known who will listen to someone's dream and not critique it. Many people will listen to your dream but will not let you finish telling about it because they are already sizing you up to it and making judgments on the odds of it happening. We need people in our lives who will just listen to our dreams and cheer us on, and such friends are special indeed.

It was natural for me, growing up as a preacher's kid, to ask a lot of questions about ministry and the role of a minister. One evening as we enjoyed our yogurt, I started to dream aloud about the kind of church I would like to pastor. I was only a preteen at the time. I asked my dad, "Dad, is it possible to build a church that would be open all the time, 24/7? The kind of church that would take in the homeless at all hours of the day and that would help people who are coming out of prison? A church that would always be on alert to help any time of the day?"

Dad looked at me and said, "I've never really heard of a church doing all that kind of work, but why don't you be the first one ever to do it." He did not understand the magnitude of what he had just said, but the Dream Center was born from that simple reassurance. He did not poke holes in my audacious scheme; he encouraged me to pursue it. (So many dreams do not see the light of the day because they get destroyed during the poking-hole phase of the vision, when the dream is imperfect or outside the bounds of normal; they die from lack of support and encouragement.)

He did not understand the magnitude of what he had just said, but the Dream Center was born from that simple reassurance. He did not poke holes in my audacious scheme; he encouraged me to pursue it.

The fact that someone I respected thought that this kind of church was possible allowed my vision to transition from a small thought to a real possibility. So much good can happen in the world if we allow small thoughts to gain momentum. On the other hand, sadly, so much good can die before it can even have a chance to develop if good ideas get discouraged.

Thus the tremendous value of each small thought—any one of them can develop into big dreams, and those dreams can come true.

I was a young man with a small seed of a thought and no way to pull it off. I did not need a complete answer that day in the yogurt shop, just a sounding board and the encouragement of someone who would not throw cold water on an idealistic concept.

Small Thoughts = Life-Changers

Earlier in the book, we talked about following the nudge and learning to trust the good things God asks us to do that are out of the ordinary. We talked about living on a divine mission every day and surrendering to the little nudges we receive daily to do good. The reason why it is so important to respond to these nudges is that one small thought could change your life.

Back when I was a child, my vision was not for a hospital or for everything else that we are doing today. It was just a dream in raw, basic form that needed encouragement.

I am dismayed by seeing how many parents speak harshly to their children about their aspirations and dreams. Even if a child's dream does not seem practical or possible, a parent does not have to discourage it. What matters the most is that home becomes a safe place to dream—a laboratory of possibility, an open door of faith. One small thought can change (for better or for worse) a school, a community, a church or anything. The first small steps must be protected. As God's people who want their kids to live by faith, we must be promoters and encouragers of faith.

A seed of doubt sowed into someone's life can become a major barrier

> One small thought can change (for better or for worse) a school, a community, a church or anything.

135

to progress. We must also protect ourselves from personal doubt-peddlers who say things such as, "It's never been done that way before," or "What makes you think you can be the first to do it?" Or they may say, "What makes you think that you are equipped to do that?"

Which brings me to another point: the idea that lack of experience or education should disqualify a person from fulfilling his or her dream. God has given me the honor of speaking at many colleges, and after I speak, during the question-and-answer session, I always get the same question: "What kind of experience did you have in cross-cultural studies?" The answer is none. But that has not disqualified me. I tell them they do not have to be uptight about that part. I may have had no experience of cross-cultural studies, but I discovered that perseverance and consistency of love are what really relate to a community in need. I tell students that determining to stay somewhere in order to love and serve the community will outlast the negative forces of the urban war for hearts and minds. I tell them to let their compassion and desire to make a difference grow and to hold on to the vision that grew from one small thought.

Dangerous Church

Our church building is located in a very unchurched community. Within steps of the church you can find marijuana shops, nightclubs and a lot of homeless people. This part of Los Angeles looks nothing like the Bible Belt or even like nearby Orange County. It is one of the toughest places in America to minister to.

For years, I tried to build the kind of church that people would drive to from the other parts of the city. That was a mistake. Here you cannot build a church based on the model of the American middle-class church. We did not have the land, the facilities or the surroundings to build a church on the familiar model of ministering to Christian families in a safe environment. We tried to do it, but copying everyone else made us a faded copy of an existing model.

One day a small, crazy thought entered my mind—to build a church that would attract people from all over the city purely *because* it was messy, even dangerous, and unlike anything that had ever been done. I decided to go one hundred percent in the direction of "Come to church, not because it's safe but because it's dangerous." The thought did not make sense in the beginning, but the more we told stories of people from the street and how their lives were being changed, the more people from all over the surrounding area began to drive to church in the heart of Los Angeles.

Families were bringing their kids to children's church where they were with kids who rode the buses from the public housing projects. Sometimes kids we bused to church would cuss in children's church, and I thought the parents would not bring their kids back, but they did. The motto of the church became "Come back to the city, and let's rebuild it." Families would drive an hour and leave their safe neighborhoods for the inconvenience and unsightliness of downtown and its graffiti-covered walls.

A simple nudge to build the church in a different way turned the tide for the entire church. It is a good example of following the nudge to do good, even when

> A simple nudge to build the church in a different way turned the tide for the entire church. It is a good example of following the nudge to do good, even when it does not make logical sense, and just figure out later how to carry it out.

it does not make logical sense, and just figure out later how to carry it out. There are so many incredible things that God can give us if we just trust those small thoughts. Those seeds can blossom into something beautiful.

A Small Thought Grows Bigger

Here is a true story that perfectly illustrates this idea. A man who had traveled all the way from Houston checked into our recovery program. He had only a small bag of clothes, and all he had on his feet were small pull-on inserts from a pair of shoes. We immediately tried to remedy this problem by going to our thrift store to find him some shoes, only to find that we did not have any in size 20. So we received a grown man into our very active one-year program—with no shoes.

A man who has been on staff for fifteen years said, "Maybe if I got word out, someone will help." He sent a text message to a friend of the Dream Center named Justin Turner, who plays third base for the Los Angeles Dodgers. It was just a thought; maybe it would work. He put the request out, but Justin Turner did not have any shoes. However, he acted on that one small thought, and it grew. Justin started to talk to the guys in the Dodger locker room about this situation and there was one other guy who wore a size 20, and he was so moved to hear about how this man had traveled from another state to come to our rehab program that he called his sponsor, Nike, and told them, "We need to get this guy some shoes."

The locker room chatter turned into "What can we do to help our brother in need?" And 24 hours later this shoeless man was having his picture taken with Dodger players, and they hand-delivered five new pairs of top-of-the line Nike shoes, the kind that only the pros wear.

The story does not end there. That night the Dodgers spent part of an inning on the broadcast talking about this unfolding string of miracles, and the entire City of Angels was blessed to hear the story of one small step by our staff member that led to a day a homeless man will never forget. You have heard the line "Bad news travels fast." It is true, but good news travels even faster.

Captive Thoughts

A mind centered on Christ is a mind that focuses on doing good. The Bible tells us to cast down "imaginations, and every high thing that exalteth itself against the knowledge of God, and bringing into captivity every thought to the obedience of Christ" (2 Corinthians 10:5 KJV). "Imaginations" and "high things" are everyday matters of life that try to present themselves as being bigger than imitating Christ. They command our attention in various ways, and they cause us to fail to respond in faith regarding a worthy undertaking that we are capable of doing.

One way we can cast down imaginations and every high thing that exalts itself against the knowledge of God and bring into captivity every thought is to follow through with the small thoughts that emerge from our reading of the Bible. For example, we can capture our upset or offended thoughts and choose to lay them down, thus freeing ourselves up to dream and creating more mental space to do good because we no longer have such a clutter of bitterness.

I was amused when I came across this Scripture one day because it mirrors what we go through in everyday life (and in all my years, I had never noticed it before!): "Do not pay attention to every word people

> You have heard the line "Bad news travels fast." It is true, but good news travels even faster.

say, or you may hear your servant cursing you—for you know in your heart that many times you yourself have cursed others" (Ecclesiastes 7:21–22). In other words, we must be careful what we allow into our thoughts, and we must demonstrate a level of grace with others, because we have all been ungracious with our words. Giving grace away is so important for both our souls and our minds. Much good can occur when we protect our thought life and maintain an active mind that is on a mission, looking for ways to do good rather than remaining embroiled in anger and frustration.

> We must demonstrate a level of grace with others, because we have all been ungracious with our words. Giving grace away is so important for both our souls and our minds.

Not only does what we choose to focus on determine what we become but so does what we choose to ignore. Show me what you do not let sink in, and I will show you the freedom you will have to love, serve and give. Every step of the way at the Dream Center we have been told that we cannot do what we are doing. In our decades of needing a miracle every day, the secret has not been in trying to prove people wrong who say we cannot do something. The secret is to choose to ignore any limiting thought that would exalt itself larger than God's love for the city. God loves Los Angeles more than I do, and I must throw the seed of doubt over the wall, away from the soil of my mind, so that it cannot take root.

Every day we are surrounded by "can't." People bound by years of addiction wonder if they can ever be free. They even question their ability to finish our program. They certainly do not need a pastor who tells them, "You can't. You're too far gone." They need a pastor that ignores what cannot be done and shouts daily about what will be done. Vison is shaped by what you choose to ignore. It is so much easier to deny a small negative thought the room to grow than it is to allow it to take root—and then to go through years and years of healing to repair the damage.

Baby Steps

One small thought is like a baby taking its first steps. The baby will stumble, stagger and fall, but you can see that the potential is there to run one day. Give your little thought, the seed of your dream, enough room to move a little bit. And in turn, give others the chance to move when they feel they have a call of God upon their lives.

One of the things I love to do when I preach is throw an idea against the wall to see if it sticks. My leadership style is not to develop a perfect plan and then launch a fancy marketing plan. I like to throw out a need and just see who will step up.

One night after a Thursday night service I saw people lining up down the street to get into a nightclub next to our church. I was frustrated that we would leave church and just walk right by the line and not have a chance to minister to them. In the middle of the message, I just threw out the idea: "Can anyone come up with a way to serve the people standing in line and show Jesus to them?"

> One small thought is like a baby taking its first steps. The baby will stumble, stagger and fall, but you can see that the potential is there to run one day.

Immediately after church a man came up to me and said, "Pastor, I can set up a DJ station, and we can play cool music and give them water and pray for the people in line if they want it." It was a pretty good, out-of-the-box idea. But the best idea came from a woman who told me she had a taco truck that she had bought years before and for whatever reason did not use anymore. It was a big truck with a kitchen that could make a lot of food. Her idea was to take the truck and park it outside the nightclub and when people came out of the club to give them free tacos. Patrons at the club might have had a few too many drinks and need a place to rest and deal with the hangover through food—and everyone loves tacos. The best way I can describe this ministry is to call it the "hangover ministry." Park a taco truck, put out some lawn chairs, let people eat for free and invite loving people to minister to them at whatever level they want to be ministered to: food, prayer, tacos, a ride home, maybe even a place to stay at the Dream Center.

When the idea was proposed after church, I got so excited about the hangover ministry. Whenever you love people in a low place, it is memorable. That is what Jesus does for us: He loves us through the hangovers of life.

My dream now is to have taco hangover trucks all over the city of Los Angeles. I want us to be there for people about whom the church has always said, "We have no open door." In truth, every door is open and everything is possible. But we must walk through those open doors and entertain the possibilities of what can be done. Life is too short to hold back. Let's venture out to see where a God-inspired idea can lead.

Again, it is like a curious baby that just learned to walk. Toddlers will wander around the house and find things that you thought they could never find. They will open doors that were closed, look under furniture and find things, maybe even discover something that you have not seen for years, simply because they are looking in spaces you have not explored for years. They freely live a life of curiosity and wonder.

No Retirement Plan

The older we get the more we need to remind ourselves not to just wait out the clock and pat ourselves on the back that we have lived a decent life. God wants us to continually push what can be done and to entertain the seeds of new ideas that would challenge us to grow.

I know what it is like to entertain a beautiful ministry idea and see it take wings. I have also been on the other side where I have opened myself up to the idea of quitting. I never sent a resignation letter to the office; I have always kept going about my regular routine. But in my heart I have had a romance with ideas about what my life could be like if I were doing something else. It is a sad place to be when your heart is only half into its assignment. You can quit and still not quit. We can sort of navigate through our days, faking it. Inside we may have thrown in the towel already, though officially we have not resigned. We are still alive but not really living. "But she that liveth in pleasure is dead while she liveth" (1 Timothy 5:6 KJV). One small thought can make us drift away from the joy of our calling and take us away from the beauty of the moment.

I know a pastor whose church failed to acknowledge him during Pastor Appreciation Month. On social media he could see all the churches that took time out of their services to honor their pastors, and in his church he was not ever recognized. He was greatly offended. He let that offense grow in his mind to the point that he started to live with a chip on his shoulder, and his ministry suffered. One day I told him, "Don't ever worry about not being recognized. Everything you do is unto the Lord and anything you get from man is a bonus." He took it to heart and focused on that one thought, and it turned his entire ministry around. I did not think the statement was very profound, but to him it was. The pastor started to meditate on this concept of doing everything unto God, and he became consumed with making God happy. He never sought appreciation from his congregation ever again. His ministry was a vertical one; now he was doing everything unto God. As a result, the joy of his calling was invigorated. One bad thought almost killed his ministry, but one small revelation became the mantra of his life.

When we live in wonder before God, we live our lives looking around every corner for possibilities. In contrast, when we are spiritually dead, we look for the next shoe to drop, anticipating trouble and fearing tragedy. God is always throwing good seed into our lives. The foundation of our calling continues to grow when we choose to live excited about tomorrow.

> When we live in wonder before God, we live our lives looking around every corner for possibilities. . . . The foundation of our calling continues to grow when we choose to live excited about tomorrow.

It is not always grand ideas and dreams and visions. Sometimes, it is just letting a thought of daily kindness grow. Allow appreciation to lightly fertilize the soil of your heart. Spend as little as five minutes a day being intentional about recognizing the good that people are doing around you. When you notice the Bible that has been sitting on your table for years, collecting dust, pick it up and brush off that dust. Let that little thought that tells you to start reading the Bible come to life. Just start reading a chapter at a time. Step out and do the good things that pop up in your thoughts. Do not harness those ideas to your doubts or fears; go with them.

Making It Personal

As I close this chapter, I must confess something. When you write a book, you share experiences and insights you have learned in hopes of encouraging the reader. However, sometimes you write a chapter and recognize your own weakness in an area that you are writing about. In this chapter I have been explaining about letting a good thought come to life by giving it more time and attention so that it can create new patterns of life. I think I need to take my own advice.

In my marriage, my wife and I are very different people. Her love language is physical touch, cuddling and holding. My love language is words of affirmation. When we buy a new bed, she wants the smaller queen-size bed so we can be close together. I want the California king bed so I can have space. I want to have so much space that when I wake up in the morning I need a megaphone to talk to my wife. And even when I am sleeping in a big bed with her, I sleep on the very edge because I do not like to be close to anyone when I sleep. I think you are getting the point: I like my space. I am not the hugging-and-holding type of husband, but my wife is the cuddling kind of wife. Amazingly, we have been married for decades, even with such polarizing qualities. We love each other, and I think she realizes that I might not ever fully meet her need. That is true of life in general; no human being will ever completely fulfill our need to feel loved. But that does not mean we do not try to fill the voids in people's lives.

Selfishness is the only word to describe how I have lived in this area of my life. If my wife needs something positive from me, why not just give it to her? Why can I not give up my selfishness, meet her need and stop trying to explain why I cannot do it? One small thought came to my mind: *I'm going to start cuddling every night.* I did not tell her this (although now it is being revealed in this book) that I intended to hold her for five minutes every night. That is what I have been doing. I even timed it by looking at the clock over her shoulder. She needed something from me, and I decided to start giving it to her, not explaining it away or making excuses about not being a "holder." After five minutes, I kiss her and roll over to the other side of our massive bed that is the size of the state of California. That five minutes is enough to make a big difference in our marriage. My wife does not need an hour of holding; a mere five minutes produces so much joy in her life. For years, my unwillingness to cuddle at bedtime was limiting how close we could become in our marriage. How ridiculous. Allowing that one small idea to come to life has done more for our marriage than the best sermons preached from our pulpit.

> What is the one thought holding you back? Just give it up. What is the one thought that will set you free? Just give it permission to take flight and watch what happens.

What is the one thought holding you back? Just give it up. What is the one thought that will set you free? Just give it permission to take flight and watch what happens. We do not have to accept the same kind of life forever. We have the power to make decisions and a great God to empower us to live challenged for so much more.

Never underestimate the power of one small thought!

MY SMALL STEP 9

After reading about this step and taking some time to pray, write down the small step you will take to follow God's nudge.

STEP 10

The Attitude of a Servant

One day I was speaking to a packed-out room at a church conference about outreach. I explained all the outreaches at the Dream Center and how to do many of the programs. At the end of the session, a pastor asked, "How do you start a food ministry in your church?" I told the audience to take careful notes because I was about to give them truth:

Step #1 Go to food pantry in your house.
Step #2 Find food in pantry.
Step #3 Put food in grocery bag.
Step #4 Take food and give it to hungry person.

At first he looked at me as if I had just delivered a deep truth, and then he smiled as if to say, "Okay, I understand. It really is that simple."

You do not have to look far to find a need. Just look everywhere, because there are needs all around us. But having the heart of a compassionate servant—now that is a different thing, and it is not so easy to find.

Jesus had compassion, and we can love others the way He did. The Bible says, "When he saw the crowds, he had compassion on them, because they were harassed and helpless, like sheep without a shepherd" (Matthew 9:36). Jesus expressed compassion by putting Himself in situations that required a response. He allowed Himself to go where there was need.

> Jesus expressed compassion by putting Himself in situations that required a response. He allowed Himself to go where there was need.

Do Not Hold Back

We are capable of doing so much good. However, many times we push our compassion down. Fear holds us back from making an uplifting remark. Weariness dulls our responses.

In my own life, I have held back compassion because I was simply too tired to extend myself. I forget that serving others energizes me, even when it is taxing. Have you ever tried to go one full day of putting others' needs in front of your own? I mean one *full* day. It is the hardest and yet most energizing thing you can do. The more we grow in Christ the more aware we are of just how much of the flesh needs to be uprooted in us. Next time you want to turn off the compassion switch, I challenge you to keep it on.

One day a pastor was in town and he wanted to hang out, so I got tickets to go see a Lakers game together. (That was back when the Lakers were good.) Our seats were almost on the court, near where the celebrities sit. I was excited to show him the Hollywood life. In the special section in which we were seated, a waiter would come and take your refreshments order right there at the seat. This was going to be great.

The game started, and within the first two minutes, the pastor took out his pen and paper and said, "Can I ask you a few questions about ministry?"

The first thing that came to my mind was, *Are you kidding me? Here at the game? How selfish are you?* But I had to do the pastoral thing and answer a few questions. I tried to pay attention to the game, but he never once looked at the court.

Instead, he stared me straight in the eye and asked me another question: "If you had to do it all over again in ministry what would you change?" My first internal response was, *Not take you to the game!* (I thought that but never said it because it does not count if you do not say it out loud, right?) He asked question after question, riveted by everything I was saying and forcing me to ignore the game. As a huge sports fan, this was torture to me.

It was a close game, down to the final couple of minutes. And did he stop? No. Just kept on asking me questions. His final question was, "Can you be my mentor?" Then he

> Living with a servant's attitude is a choice, one that we have to make every day.

began to cry as he talked about all the struggles he was going through. As much as I wanted to push aside the attitude of a servant, I could not. I had to go back and remember who I am, an ambassador for Christ. There are 82 basketball games in a season but only one moment to talk with this pastor. Many people's lives were at stake back home because of this troubled pastor.

I shook off my bad attitude and put on an attitude of a servant and said, "It would be my greatest honor to be your mentor."

Only then did he turn back to the game, exclaiming, "Can you believe how good this game is?" . . . The game I never got to see. But, hey, I had the chance to build a relationship that would keep a pastor going forward in his calling.

Living with a servant's attitude is a choice, one that we have to make every day.

Qualities of a Servant

Someone who has the attitude of a servant possesses the same qualities that we see represented in the life of Jesus.

The first quality of a servant is this: *Servants serve faithfully even while being underappreciated.* A servant desires to reflect Jesus more than to receive praise. The crowds were drawn to Jesus for miracles, and they scattered when He was done. The disciples used Him for position and authority, but He remained patient with them. When He was on the cross, only one of them stayed with Him, while the others scattered. Through everything, He glorified His Father in heaven, and there is no greater reward for faithfulness than that.

Another quality of a servant is *finding joy in dying to oneself.* The servant finds joy in emptying himself because by emptying himself, he obtains more. True servants understand that the Kingdom of God is reversed: The more you give of yourself, the less it takes to make you happy. You could say that God's servants live in an alternate universe. The core of their conviction comes from Jesus' words: "Give, and it will be given to you. A good measure, pressed down, shaken together and running over, will be poured into your lap. For with the measure you use, it will be measured to you" (Luke 6:38).

Once I was flying back to Los Angeles from Dallas on the 10:50 p.m. flight. I had just finished a wonderful church service and was so happy to be able to catch the late-night flight. Like any pastor or businessperson after a good day's work, I was basking in the satisfaction of having accomplished something well. I settled into my seat on the plane in a good mood, kind of living on a high.

I was seated next to a woman whose husband was a row behind me, and they kept talking over the row to each other. He had a middle seat and I had the coveted aisle seat. I turned to him and said, "Sir, do you want my seat so you can sit next to your wife?" He was so blown away.

He said, "You mean you would give up your aisle seat for a middle seat? For me?" When he said that, he pointed to his heart like a man undeserving.

I gave him a fist pound and said, "Come on up here and sit by your wife." He pulled out his credit card and told me he would by me any alcoholic beverage on the plane. I told him no thanks, but I did pull out a Dream Center credit card machine and asked for a donation. (Just kidding! But it would have been a good idea.)

The ironic thing was he ended up fighting with his wife, so I probably should have kept the original seat. But I wanted to show the joy of dying to yourself. It is so easy for us to protect little places of territory that do not matter. Trading seats on a plane is not a big deal in comparison to making someone's day.

> If you ask servants of Jesus to make lists of the things that make them happy, they probably could put it all on a Post-it Note. The lists are so short because they have lost themselves in serving.

A third attitude of a servant is *having no agenda except Jesus*. This is a tough one because the people around us are looking out for their personal schedules and agendas, and we fall into that pattern too easily. The daily agenda of Jesus consists of a small checklist of ways He can serve others, and our agenda should match His. If you ask servants of Jesus to make lists of the things that make them happy, they probably could put it all on a Post-it Note. The lists are so short because they have lost themselves in serving.

Serving outside of Jesus' agenda is very challenging. We all feel we are entitled to an exchange. I gave you this, you give me that. We are wired to be deal makers. Yet servants will always give more than they receive; their model is not the give-and-take of the world. Their standard is living up to the standard of the One who gave expecting nothing in return. When that is the model we are going for, we will always be satisfied with the scoreboard being uneven. In fact, instead of looking for ways to get back what we give, we look for ways the scoreboard can be even *more* uneven!

Love Does Not Keep Score

People say love does not keep score. This is true. Love does not count up what you do for someone and what they do for you in return, contemplating an equal exchange. True love is extreme; it wants the score to be in the other side's favor and does not mind the lopsided margin.

If I had started the Dream Center to get the appreciation of man, I would have quit a long time ago. There were a few times I wanted to quit in the early stages, and it was always because I was keeping score. I did something for someone, and therefore I should get a certain kind of reward. I built a free place for homeless people, and therefore I should get a fair share of recognition. The desire to quit always came because I was disappointed about not getting back equal value from what I had given.

The antidote to this attitude was to study the life of Jesus and to see how He lived empty and yet full at the same time. Seeing this made me *want* to give much more than I got in return. The thing that had disappointed me the most became the very thing I wanted. I wanted to tilt the uneven scales even more to the others' advantage.

In a funny way, a selfish life can have value—if it makes you realize that it is not what you wanted. That is why you hear stories of people who lost it all and went to prison and then when they come out they say, "That is the best thing that ever happened in my life." I have met people who were making a lot of money before they went to prison. When they get out and begin to work for minimum wage at the Dream Center, they consider those the best years of their life. For them, the scales tipped from getting to giving, and that became a healing thing.

> We preach about achieving balance in our lives, but there is one area in which life should be imbalanced, and that is in serving. Give more than you receive.

We preach about achieving balance in our lives, but there is one area in which life should be imbalanced, and that is in serving. Give more than you receive and you will live a happy, imbalanced life, free from the trap of finding your happiness only in receiving approval and material things.

Generosity is more than just an act; it is a way of thinking, a way of seeing and a way of living. As the proverb explains,

> There is one who scatters and yet increases more; and there is one who withholds more than is right, but it leads to poverty. The generous soul will be made rich, and he who waters will also be watered himself.
>
> Proverbs 11:24–25 NKJV

A generous person has the attributes of a servant. What will be enriched in a life that is generous to the core? The soul of a generous person will be made rich. A life of giving is a life of wealth, on the inside.

Good Steward or Good Servant?

When the attributes of a servant take over in your life, you start doing strange things. You might find yourself pulling up to a fast-food drive-thru and paying for the order of the people behind you, people you do not even know. Or you may be the first one to volunteer when your kids' school team needs a driver. The pattern of your life becomes generous, and you start doing your daily-life routines from the joy of laying down your own life, gradually moving away from catering to your own needs.

Here is an interesting example: As I was writing this chapter, I did not want to interrupt the flow, so I took out my phone and ordered some food on the Postmates app. (Postmates is a delivery service you can use with a few taps on your phone. Then you do not have to go anywhere; somebody will bring your order to you.) I would like to tell you that I ordered something healthy, but that would be a lie. I ordered Popeye's chicken. All the places I could have ordered from, and I chose the greasy chicken. Now, what I had just written about living generously had gotten deep into my spirit, and it made me want to intentionally live what I had been writing. A woman came to my door to deliver the food, and she was so nice. Normally, I give the standard tip through the Postmates app, but this time I handed her a twenty-dollar bill. She broke down in tears and thanked me. She told me that this was going to help her buy diapers for her kids. It made her day, and it made my day even better.

I went back into the house, reflecting on that powerful moment. Then I repented after doing something right. What? I did something nice for someone and then I repented instead of going back to my room jumping up and down and celebrating that I had gotten it right for once? I repented to God for overthinking compassion. I knew I had tried to talk myself out of giving that tip. I kept thinking about how reckless it felt, how the cost of the meal was only nine dollars, way out of proportion to a twenty-dollar tip. Then I thought of the favorite Christian rationale, "Am I being a good steward?"

Well, I am here to tell you that anytime you do something for others and against your flesh, it is good stewardship. The greatest obstacle that blocks the attitude of a servant is pride. Our flesh says, "I need my fair share. If I give this much in a relationship, I should expect to get a certain amount back." Our pride does not like the idea of being shortchanged or of getting the low end of the bargain. And yet we cannot see or touch our pride, which makes it an elusive target. So all we can do is repent when we catch ourselves trying to rationalize our actions based on what they can do for us.

> Anytime you do something for others and against your flesh, it is good stewardship. The greatest obstacle that blocks the attitude of a servant is pride.

The world will never give you the respect you want, and even your family will not give you enough respect. By nature, pride makes you expect the people around you to give honor or life back to you. You cannot control what they give to you. But you can control what you give to them! You can adopt the attitude of a servant and live proactively, beautifully lost in purpose. You can control your happiness by what you give, and guaranteed, you will get back a reward in proportion to whatever you give.

Think Differently

Servants just think differently. That is what Caleb did. When he believed God's promise, God said of him: "My servant Caleb thinks differently and follows me completely" (Numbers 14:24 NCV). God is always a rewarder of *why* we do something as much as *what* we do. Far from using serving as part of a negotiation strategy to get what we want, a real servant simply allows God to use his or her life for what He wants.

But people with a servant's heart are rare. Even the apostle Paul struggled to find someone with an attitude of a servant. In fact, Timothy was the only one he could use as an illustration. Self-gratification versus self-denial—I think this is the greatest war we face. And God gives us plenty of tests to see how we are doing.

Think of the ultimate act of humility in the Bible, the time when Jesus washed the feet of His disciples. The imagery of this picture is truly stunning: the Savior of the world bending over to wash the dirty feet of the disciples after miles of travel. Jesus could do this because He was secure in who He was and knew His identity. He did not need to earn humility points to prove anything, and neither do we.

The more insecure you are, the more approval you want from the world. You only become more secure when you realize that your life is not your own and you live for the Lord's approval alone. Disregard the voices of the world around you. They tell you that you are right for demanding what you want, that you deserve this and that. All around us, people are fighting for their rights daily, thinking that this will buy them a secure identity.

One of the most secure people in all the Bible is James. You cannot get any better than being the half brother of Jesus. If I were James, I probably would have used my connections to Jesus to get some pretty cool things out of life. Just think, if Jesus walked on earth today, as His half brother, I would stand a very good chance of getting front-row seats to every NBA game. However, there is no record of James leveraging his family influence to go to the front of the line or for anything else. James was simply content to settle into his role, and he even called himself "a servant of God and of the Lord Jesus Christ" (James 1:1). He found his identity in being close to Jesus and serving Him in whatever way He desired.

> The more insecure you are, the more approval you want from the world. You only become more secure when you realize that your life is not your own and you live for the Lord's approval alone.

Audience of One

Our house was going through a remodel, and my family needed a place to stay. So we decided to stay for a few months in my office at the Dream Center. My office consists of a workroom and a little getaway room attached to it that usually serves the purpose of housing guest pastors. Let's just say that it was an interesting season of our lives. Most of the 250 men in our recovery program lived on the hospital floor below my office. It is not easy for a family of four to adjust from living in a house to being squeezed into an office. I got frustrated at how slowly the progress on the house was moving along, given the requirements for a number of new permits and regulations. The project had been delayed, and it was pushing close to a year.

At the same time, we had the rewarding privilege of hearing, every night before bedtime, the men singing praises to God. Their voices echoed up from the floor below us. These former gang members and ex-convicts were all praising God in their (may I say) bad singing voices. But it was beautiful to hear. They had no cell phones and no distractions. For one year they were doing everything for the Lord. For them, everything was about Jesus. The only focus for their life was, "How can I glorify God in what I do?"

All day long, they served Jesus, and their serving completely changed their lives. Have you ever seen the television show in which some woman gets a complete makeover from a celebrity stylist? At the end of the show, there is this great reveal, and when the woman walks out, you do not even recognize her because the best stylists in the world have reshaped her image. The crowd is in awe, and people gasp at the monumental transformation. Something even better happens in the lives of people who devote all of their attention to serving Jesus. You cannot even recognize them anymore. Their focus is on Jesus to the point that they completely lose themselves in living for an audience of One.

Dr. Albert Schweitzer, who devoted his life to serving in Africa, once said, "The only really happy people are those who have learned to serve." I would take it a step further. I would say that the only true joy in life is found in narrowing everything down to serving an audience of One. We are serving Jesus as, one by one, we serve the people He has put in our lives. This makes us unusual in today's world, where success is measured in how much you move the masses.

There are many wonderful churches being built today—by hype. They develop great marketing plans and social media platforms, and some obtain the endorsement of celebrities so that they can hit the ground running in a church plant. The church-planting model in today's world is to start off big.

But one problem with social media is that it both gives and takes away. It can raise someone up and then drag that person right back down. It can create influencers and then ruin their reputations.

I can tell you from personal experience that the best way to build a church is to start with what you have, even if it is small, and just be happy with flying below the radar. Enjoy each small progress, and celebrate one small step at a time. Commit yourself to faithfulness rather than a five-year plan. Make the purpose of your success be the doing of your work unto God. If you focus on the intention of your calling more than on the growth, you will build a generational church, not just an attractional church.

The foundation should be on having the heart of a servant, not on being an overnight influencer. If you have massive early growth, then you must go deeper into the roots and foundation of your soil. The bigger the tent, the deeper the stakes need to go and the longer the ropes need to be to hold it up.

> Make the purpose of your success be the doing of your work unto God. If you focus on the intention of your calling more than on the growth, you will build a generational church, not just an attractional church.

Relentlessly build a foundation of proper motivation into your vision. In the business world, the more success you obtain, the more obligated you are to use that influence to serve those who have the least influence.

Growth, prosperity and influence should carry with them the idea that the higher you go, the lower you must intentionally go to make a difference. You must become a servant, or your success is empty.

You can do this! You can cultivate the attitude of a servant in your life by taking one step at a time toward honoring God, letting your worship and your actions shout down the noise of the world with its demands for hollow praise.

MY SMALL STEP 10

After reading about this step and taking some time to pray, write down the small step you will take to follow God's nudge.

STEP 11

The Risk-Taking Step

Back in 1984, I remember snuggling on the couch with my family watching the Orange Bowl as the Miami Hurricanes and the Nebraska Cornhuskers contended for the national championship. Tom Osborne was the coach for Nebraska, and his team was undefeated.

In those days there were no overtimes in college football. It came down to the final drive of the game, and Nebraska scored a touchdown. Now the score was 29–30. Since they were higher-ranked than Miami, all they had to do was kick for the extra point, and the game would end in a 30–30 tie, with the higher-ranked Nebraska automatically becoming the national champion. Then every one of those college players would forever be known as a national champion.

But what happened is that, instead of going for the extra point and a tie, Coach Osborne decided to go for the win with a two-point conversion—and Nebraska lost the national championship. After the game, a very stoic Osborne was asked why he did not take the guaranteed national title by kicking for the extra point. His answer was simple: "I don't think you go for the tie in that case. You always try to win the game." He took a risk and he lost.

I was watching a replay of that game the other day, and the thought hit me: If he had gone for the tie, he would have been criticized, but when he went for the win, he was criticized. You might as well go for the win in such a situation, because either way people are going to talk about you. Even if you try to avoid risk, you will end up receiving criticism.

Go for the Win

You might as well go for the win, even if you fail. Some people will not get married because they are afraid of risk. But walking in blind faith feels risky, too. The Bible says, "We walk by faith, not by sight" (2 Corinthians 5:7 NKJV). Depending upon natural things for security creates a false illusion of security, and it lures us into dullness. We will never be useful to God unless we are willing to take risks.

Joshua got up before three million Jews, opened his mouth and said, "Sun, stand still!" (Joshua 10:12). Had he gone a little crazy? Maybe the pressure of leadership had finally gotten him. You know when someone makes a statement like that, people are going to watch the sun. He dared to take that risk, and it worked. The sun stood still.

Faith is when you put it on the line. When we bought the Queen of Angels Hospital, everyone thought we were crazy. They did not say we were making a risk-taking step—they thought we were walking the plank! We had $1,500 a week coming into our offering plates, and we had made an offer on a building that cost four million dollars. People called us irresponsible and reckless, and they told us we had missed God. We could have played it safe in that first church building that we had inherited, but instead we went for the win.

Too often, people think that when they can do something and the pieces fit together "it must be God," because it works. However, that is not how you determine His will. The best way to follow Him is to have pure intentions. Taking a risk out of selfish motivation feels scary, but when the mission is not flooded with selfish ambition, it seems clearer, and the risk feels possible.

In my vocabulary, taking a risk is spiritual and playing it safe is carnal. Taking a risk for God could mean taking a risk on someone who has burned every bridge, or taking a risk on an idea that could help people. Such risk-taking is spiritual because you have invited God into the equation.

When I was a skinny twig playing football, my dad used to tell me that standing around is how you will get hurt. He told me that the safest place to be is right there in the pile. You must do something, step out in faith, and most often that means taking the risk of trusting in blind faith.

I have known people who are still waiting after years for a confirmation to do something. It is like they need an angel or a marching band from heaven to come down and announce God's will in an elaborate way. But it did not always work that way in the Bible, did it? There is no way around risk. Abraham by faith went to a land where he had never gone before and did not even know where he was going. He took the plunge; he was willing to walk the plank, and the only assurance he had was God telling him, "If you go, I'll go."

God Is with You

Let me challenge you with this bold statement: *Make it up as you go.* You cannot walk by faith and seek security at the same time. There is no reason to ask God for something if you will not act on what you hear from Him.

The only sign you need is the persistent passion for something that God places in your heart. When He stirs your heart to do something,

He will be with you. Notice the words "the Lord worked with them" in Mark 16:20: "Then the disciples went out and preached everywhere, and the Lord worked with them and confirmed his word by the signs that accompanied it." They needed God along the way because nothing was safe; what they were doing was dangerous business. How wonderful it is to know that we, too, can have total assurance of God's help. When we set out to do God's will, He will work with us along the way.

This applies to all sorts of endeavors. When you have that hard conversation with someone, God is with you. When you face the long road back from failure and seek to rise again, God is with you. Hope might die for a short while, but do not let tomorrow die. You will never know what tomorrow could have been unless you take the plunge. God will help you sort everything out.

Tune out the overcautious voices from your own mind and from others that will hold you back from taking a risk, and give God a chance to do something. Remember the faith of Noah. *The Message* puts it in clear words: "By faith, Noah built a ship in the middle of dry land. He was warned about something he couldn't see, and acted on what he was told. The result? His family was saved" (Hebrews 11:7, referring to the story in Genesis 6–9). Let's stop and take another look at those words. Noah's family was saved because he did something bold that to him surely seemed risky. He believed every word that God spoke and worked incredibly hard to follow through, in blind, courageous faith. He had an aggressive nature, but he did not trust his own instincts. Instead, he trusted a very outside-the-box word that told him to build an ark according to exact specifications, even though he had never seen one before, and to stock it with provisions and animals according to exact specifications. It took him years just to build the ark, and the whole time he did not see any results. In fact, he faced ridicule, fatigue and (I would imagine) doubts. But he carried through—and his willingness to take a faith-risk saved his family. Faith is not as unsafe as we think it is. In fact, the safest place to be is in the will of God. Your risky-feeling faith step could be a lifesaving step.

Let's continue reading about Noah in *The Message*, still from verse 7 of Hebrews 11: "His act of faith drew a sharp line between the evil of the unbelieving world and the rightness of the believing world." His faith in building the ark was an act of righteousness. All around him, the people were living it up and enjoying wild living while Noah steadily labored along. He pleased God every single day as he assembled piece after piece of that floating vessel. His faith-based actions were in direct contrast to the activities of the world around him. None of them understood his faith, and they thought

> Faith is not as unsafe as we think it is. In fact, the safest place to be is in the will of God.

he was wasting his time. It was even pleasing to God that Noah's faith was misunderstood. God wants all of us to live our lives in such a wonderful, trusting way that it will often be misunderstood. (This does not only pertain to visionary acts of courage but to everyday ordinary activities in our lives.)

The verse finishes off by saying, "As a result, Noah became intimate with God." Any journey with God that requires faith and total abandonment to His purposes will produce intimacy with God. Noah did not surrender to the disobedience and sin of the culture around him. He chose to go on a journey of faith with God. He chose to go for the win daily and not settle for the tie. He kept taking the risky, uncertain steps that would bring him close to God.

It is something like what happens with veterans who serve in combat together. It is amazing to see the incredible bond that exists between them long after they return to their homes. The years pass by, and as these men and women grow old, many of them never lose contact with each other. Being in the trenches together has bonded them forever; that shared hardship creates a unity that can never be broken. In a similar way, Noah was bonded with God because he had chosen to take such a demanding journey of faith. He needed God to stay by his side from beginning to end.

Dancing Lloyd

There is a man who comes to our church named Lloyd. He has been coming to our church ever since it first opened its doors. He is known as Dancing Lloyd. He is an older man, and he wears dress pants, a vest and a top hat every day. I have never seen Lloyd not spruced up.

Lloyd does not have much money, and he has been through trauma in his life, but this man lives his life enthusiastically. He is always on the move, and he is always coming to church. He will travel many miles to get to church. In fact, one time I got a phone call from the hospital from Lloyd. He wanted to apologize to me for missing church because he broke his arm.

He spends most of his time walking the streets of Los Angeles, dancing around town to the beat of his own drum and reflecting the love of Jesus like the sunshine. Lloyd loves the Lord with every ounce of energy he has. Just seeing him puts my faith in perspective immediately.

Lloyd loves God, he has always got praise in his heart, and his feet are quick to dance in darkness. I think of all the times I have seen Dancing Lloyd walking along the dangerous streets of Los Angeles at night just to catch another bus on his way home. Honestly, I am amazed something tragic has not happened to him, because he would seem to be so vulnerable to mugging. Downtown Los Angeles is not exactly the retirement capital of the world. Lloyd is a joyful old man minding his own business, and I should stop fearing for his safety, because he is completely free from fear. It must be wonderful to be so clueless to danger and so alive to every step that you take. Dancing Lloyd knows he is alive to bring joy to the world, and that purpose alone preserves him from danger. I will go as far as to say that he is safer in the back alleys of Los Angeles than a wealthy billionaire in a mansion in Beverly Hills who lives to obtain more possessions that cannot save him.

I remember one year we had a little family-friendly New Year's Eve dance party at the church. Of course, Lloyd showed up. Lloyd was the oldest guy on the dance floor that night by decades. In the middle of the night, he danced so hard that he passed out. His heart was beating too quickly and everyone thought he was having a heart attack. We rushed him over to the corner to cool him down and get him some water, and we were getting ready to take him to the emergency room. But ten minutes later, he dusted off his suit and went right back out on the floor to dance the night away. He just keeps going on and on, and he is probably going to outlive us all. We get a certain kind of joy from a person who just lives life in the joy of the Lord and does not try to make sense of everything.

There is only one Dancing Lloyd—and there is only one you. We all have unique gifts, and God gave them to us so that we could help change the world around us. But we need to use them. Open up to God and do not hold back the incredible abilities He has given you. Resist the culture around you, which will try to lure you into conformity. Do not let that happen. Ask God to help you discover the gifting He has given you, and be unashamed to pour yourself out. Scripture tells us, "Do not conform to the pattern of this world, but be transformed by the renewing of your mind. Then you will be able to test and approve what God's will is—his good, pleasing and perfect will" (Romans 12:2). Create a new pattern or design to give the world and refuse to fit yourself into any mold except the unique one that God created for you. Never grow out of your childlike joy in walking (or dancing!) with your loving Father.

King Saul's Heavy Burden

King Saul was trapped within himself, battling incredible depression and more. David came in and played the harp to try to get him out of his foul mood. I think one of the reasons for Saul's hatred of David was that David was everything Saul wished he could be, and he was both jealous and intimidated by the contrast between them. As David was playing the harp, Saul had suddenly had enough. He took a javelin and threw it at David. David escaped harm and went away, never to play his harp for the king again (see 1 Samuel 18:10–13).

Saul was trapped within himself. Needless to say, he had lost all sense of wonder and adventure. His life had become fear-filled. A survival mentality had set in. He saw danger around every corner, and the world he lived in became smaller. All hope of a brighter day diminished. You and I can fall into a similar state if we are not careful.

Stuck in a place of melancholy, King Saul became intimidated by everything. He was living the old proverb that says, "Satan delights to fish in troubled waters." The major source of intimidation in his life was no longer enemy armies, but himself. His melancholy spirit turned into a tormenting spirit. He was unwilling to change, stuck in himself. He could not get out of his own head. He was performing his governmental duties on autopilot and in fear rather than in purposeful faith. What a contrast from the man who was so humble he went and hid behind the luggage when he was called out to be a king. Now, he was trapped with his own thoughts in a twisted world of self-preservation.

It is not only the King Sauls of the world who end up like this. It is fully possible for any one of us to drift into a place where we are afraid to take the risk of faith. We fail to forgive for so long, or to do something that requires faith, that we settle for a world of existing rather than living.

Saul possessed a bitter spirit, and he was full of his own pride. He was also adept at using various mechanisms to protect himself. He could have taken David in as a son and raised him up for great things. He could have been a proactive, capable leader. But no, he let fear and control (which always go hand in hand) take over his thoughts.

Fear should have been dealt with early on in Saul's life, but it was not. We can learn what not to do from his example. None of us should capitulate to fear and accept it as normal. Fear is passive, corrosive and completely opposed to the joy of being alive. Obviously, fear keeps us from taking risks.

Love Wins over Fear

Saul may have been the king, but he operated under a burden of fear. By listening to half-truths (*David is stronger than I am; therefore his very presence threatens my existence.* . . .), he undermined his own leadership ability. Instead of serving others *through* his burden of fear, which might have allowed him to treat David as a son and ally, he allowed his fearfulness to rule—and he attacked his own anointed successor. If only he had recognized his fear and countered it by reaching out to David, his every step of love would have not only blessed David and his son Jonathan and everyone else, but his actions would have aggressively combated his own fears.

Every risk that we take relationally for the cause of Christ does one important thing—it keeps us relying on God. Saul played it safe, which proved to be a dangerous move because he allowed his mind to go in the direction of bitterness and self-containment. Jesus, however, risked it all for love. And He showed us better than anybody that the greatest reward always comes at the end of the hardest decision of sacrifice.

How did Jesus keep enduring the torture of the cross? What kept Him going through the whippings, the beatings, the scorn, the crown of thorns? It was His active love for humanity—including the very men who were killing Him. Love kept him going, redeeming love, risk-taking love. Love allowed Him to sacrifice Himself for the men, women and children of this world, most of whom were clueless, and some of whom hated Him in return. He just kept loving, and He still does.

I am in complete awe at the testimonies I hear from people who live at the Dream Center. I marvel not only at what the people in rehab overcome but also at what they choose to forgive. When I hear their stories, sometimes the fleshly side of me says, *No, don't forgive that; that's too painful to forgive!* Then I realize that forgiving like that is bringing them alive in Christ. They forgive the unthinkable, and they choose to live in risky love. The walls around their hearts and minds come down, and they start to think like heaven, no longer conformed to the world.

Flee from Fear

One mistake we make in life is to think that somehow if we fear something, it means we are caring more, or that fear serves as a motivation for good works. For instance, I have been asked many times if the fear of failure is what kept us going forward in building the Dream Center.

The opposite is true. Fear did not stimulate the adrenaline to fire me up, and it did not create in me the will to win. No, fear was bad for me. It had me against the ropes so many times, and it almost knocked me out more than once. Fear has been my constant enemy, trying to force me back into a small corner labeled, "Play It Safe. Don't Take Risks." Fear has never contributed a single thing toward my calling. In the early years of ministry, I was so worried all the time about being a success that anxiety and fear only pushed me to failure. Success cannot be achieved in the presence of fear.

Fear is the belief that you are on your own and everything depends upon your performance.

> Fear is the belief that you are on your own and everything depends upon your performance.

Search the Bible sometime for the words *fear not* and you will be astounded by how many times that little phrase appears. God does not want us to be terrified. He knows that fear produces nothing in our lives except the very thing we are afraid of. So where did we get the notion that fear pushes people to greatness? Not from the Word of God.

Everything we do at the Dream Center is risky. The liability alone of housing hundreds of people is staggering. We can respond to the challenges either with fear or with faith. When I speak at conferences concerning risk and how to manage it, I get a lot of what I consider fear-based questions, such as, "What if [this bad thing] happens?" Fear makes us borrow trouble.

You can tell a lot about what a person is going to accomplish by the motivation behind their questions. If someone is stepping up to take on the risk of helping hurting people but that person's first thought is, *What could go wrong for me?* we know that person is not ready. He or she is missing the love motivation—and love casts out fear. The apostle John wrote, "There is no fear in love. But perfect love drives out fear, because fear has to do with punishment. The one who fears is not made perfect in love" (1 John 4:18).

If you want to step up to the challenge of loving a broken world, you cannot allow yourself to become overwhelmed with the what-ifs—the frightening things that threaten your success. You cannot give fear an inch because it is greedy and tends to occupy more and more space in your life. Or, to create a more memorable analogy: A shark will smell blood in the water and go for the attack, and fear is the same way.

Fear pushes us to operate more in the flesh to accomplish what we want to do, instead of relying on the Spirit of God to operate with freedom in our lives to accomplish His will.

The reason why I am pushing back so hard against fear is because, in my experience, it almost drove me into the ground. As the son of one of the spiritual giants in the faith, I put high expectations on myself to succeed. God did not want me to be so driven for success. I was anxious and ambitious, trying to take one giant leap every single day, but God wanted me only to learn to love in small ways. The Lord took me to the backstreets of the inner city to teach me both how to love hurting people and how to appreciate small victories and tiny acts of courageous love.

As a pastor, I would have catapulted to success so much faster if I had inherited a thriving church, but what God taught me through suffering and sleepless nights could never be matched by the adrenaline rush of a big church service or preaching on a grand stage. What I learned on the streets of Los Angeles boils down to one valuable lesson: Do everything by faith. I also learned that fear never equals love. No, fear equals the death of creativity, the death of proper motivation and the death of loftier goals that come through faith.

Love Conquers Fear

I have seen what addiction does to people, and it is terrifying. A young man will steal from his old grandparents just to get enough money to catch another high. A young woman will sell her own clothes off her back and run through the streets naked just to get one more hit of a drug. When someone goes off the deep edge of addiction, it is a terrifying thing. Yet long before someone gets to that point, fear takes deep root.

How can you keep that from happening? It cannot happen without God. Have you ever been going through a hard time in life and suddenly out of nowhere a surge of optimism and hope sweeps over you? You cannot explain it, but it captures your attention. Then it leaves after a couple of minutes. I contend that these are moments when God is sprinkling seeds of faith in your soul to remind you that His kind of life is attainable if you will choose it. With His ongoing help, it is fully possible to live by faith, allowing the awareness of Jesus Christ to permeate everything. You need to let those seeds grow in your heart and to build upon those moments. That is the way to cut off fear before it becomes an addiction.

I was watching a college football game, and at halftime the sideline reporter asked one of the coaches, "What did the other team figure out? Why are they coming back to the winning side?"

I love his answer. He said, "Nothing, they didn't figure out nothing." The reason I loved that response is he did not let the reporter try to put her fear and doubt upon him. In the same way, we need to resist making any concessions to fear. We need to hold our ground and stop fear from winning any more of the territory of our hearts. And we need to never stop taking risks when the nudge of the Holy Spirit comes.

There is a master room in a house, and there is a master room in your soul. Do not allow the enemy to reside in the master room of your soul. Christians are supposed to be humble; it is true. But that does not mean that we should remain ignorant about spiritual realities. We do not need to submit to anything that does not come from God Himself. Confidently, we can lean all of our weight (including the weight of our fears and traumas) on Him. Philippians 1:6 says, ". . . being confident of this, that he who began a good work in you will carry it on to completion until the day of Christ Jesus." We have confidence in our God's ability to start and finish everything He said He can do. We do not have to find something to fear all the time. The greatest battle of our lives will always be fear versus faith.

> The greatest battle of our lives will always be fear versus faith.

Take a Faith Challenge

You can tell from reading this book that I love challenges. A challenge changes your focus and gets you going. I especially love thirty-day challenges, because thirty days is enough time to create a real change of scenery in the landscape of your life. Weight loss, for example, is a challenge that needs at least thirty days to show some results. You need to overcome some initial barriers before the rhythm of momentum will start carrying you.

How about one more challenge—a thirty-day faith challenge? I challenge you to walk around your house for thirty days and just talk ridiculous faith. Even if it is over the top, that is totally fine. If it annoys people, that is even better. I am talking thirty days of overkill, because you cannot go too far with your faith. If you are part of a small group reading this book, you could do the challenge together.

Set aside thirty days to saturate yourself with the constant awareness of your need to live by faith. Go wild with it! Speak life and faith to your business, your workplace, your spouse, your kids, your friends at church. Walk around the office and speak belief over people. Talk about the brighter day that is coming, and just unload a barrage of encouragement. The longer we live, the more we can be vulnerable to lose faith in humanity and start to give up and conform to the culture's language. It is time to turn that around.

People might think you are on drugs, and that is what you want. We have annoyed each other too long with fear. Now it is time to annoy each other with faith. A radical faith challenge will reset your life. Such a challenge will redirect your life, as you say over and over how great God is.

One of the worst things about fear is that it puts our attention back onto ourselves. At the least, that is not a happy place to live. At the worst, we lose our way and wander away from the pathway of faith. We are at our best only when we operate in faith, when we replace our fears with faith and place ourselves in God's capable hands.

Take the challenge and become a prisoner of great expectations. Jesus said, "The thief comes only to steal and kill and destroy; I have come that that they may have life, and have it to the full" (John 10:10). The abundant life is not about having more money or being rich; it is about living full of faith and expectation, completely sold out to God's promises and fortified in His guarantees.

Live with a Faith-Filled, Get-to-Serve Mindset

I am writing this book during the 25th anniversary of the Dream Center, and writing it is making me reexamine the struggles I have encountered. The challenge to living daily with risk-taking faith means skating on the edge of failure, and after a while, that can wear a person down. It can make you want to take refuge in seemingly safe places, and it can make it much harder to see the forest for the trees. Sometimes small things can trip you up.

I have found that giving and serving year after year can make me vulnerable to falling into a trap of approaching life with a check-off-the-box attitude. I end up viewing life through the lens of "Just get through this or that and then I will be happy on the other side." For example, I am not a person who enjoys dressing up and going to functions or parties. However, my role as a pastor of what some consider a charity brings me invitations to many of these things. My wife does very well at such events, but truthfully, I find very little joy in walking around and just mingling. I will go a step further—it feels like torture. Let's say I look at my calendar on Monday and see that I have to go to a social event on the upcoming Friday night. Suddenly I lose my victory and my ability to serve with joy. Monday is ruined. Tuesday is no better, and Wednesday may be worse, as Friday draws closer. You get the idea. I lose days of fruitful and joyful serving, simply because of a Friday night party. (In using this illustration, I am probably risking not being invited to the next party.) My whole week gets ruined by something on my calendar.

Seeing this happen repeatedly got my attention. I had to look in my heart and find out why I could be happy only when such events were over. Were my faith and joy that fragile? With God's help, I came to the realization that I had fallen into a check-off-the-box attitude. Life was becoming an obligation, not a joy. I was living with a have-to-serve rather than a get-to-serve mindset.

Anyone can love life when looking forward to something they enjoy. It takes character to find ways to rise to the challenge of loving and serving with joy even when you are facing the next day with dread. When joyful anticipation does not come naturally, what can you do?

In this case, I had to recognize that someone was trying to show his or her love and appreciation by arranging this social event and that it was selfish of me to see it as just one more unpleasant thing on my calendar. In fact, it was time for me to learn to love doing things that do not come naturally—and to stop caving in to my personal preferences. In other words, I could make it part of my faith challenge.

After all, life is full of preferences and choices, and we do not all enjoy the same things. So why not choose to lay down my preferences and decide to value what other people love even though it might not be my cup of tea?

This does not apply only to me and mingling at parties. In your marriage, you can draw much closer together if you step out to participate in something your spouse enjoys. Take a risky step and go outside of your comfort zone. You might hate baseball but your husband loves it. So go with him to a game and let him discuss strategies and teams with you. Ask questions. Respect his grasp of his favorite sport. Do that, and be amazed at how much your communication will open up. Sure, you may never care deeply about baseball. But you care about communication with your husband, and this is one way to improve it. What made you think that true communication must be deep and mutually satisfying? Yes, in too many movies the man or the woman always has the perfect thing to say in an awkward situation. But remember that those are scripted lines they have memorized and not real life. I have found, quite simply, that if you want to get into deeper communication with somebody (not only your spouse), you must lay the foundation of being willing to discuss something the other person enjoys.

Serve with All Your Might

One of my favorite verses in the Bible is Ecclesiastes 9:10, which advises: "Whatever your hand finds to do, do it with all your might." Whatever is on your schedule, do it with all your might. Whatever you might not look forward to, do it with all your might. There is no way around it; you must give your all, all the time.

God wants us to look at everything we encounter as an opportunity to worship Him by giving it our best. I will never naturally love everything I am called to do, but I am obligated to give it my best. We glorify God to the utmost when we choose to stay where conditions are not what we prefer. It is part of having a risk-taking spirit, and it applies to every area of our lives.

> "Whatever your hand finds to do, do it with all your might."

Leave your comfort zone and open your life to new territory. Take risks and expand the boundaries of your life. Challenge the boundaries of what you prefer for the sake of making life better for others. It is worth it every time.

MY SMALL STEP 11

After reading about this step and taking some time to pray, write down the small step you will take to follow God's nudge.

STEP 12

Step to the Future

One night at church a man in our recovery program was giving a testimony about what had brought him to the Dream Center. It was a wild story full of drug addiction and living on the streets, the story of a man who totally gave up on life. He told how one night he was on the run from the cops. In his desperation to get away, he jumped into a garbage can outside the home of one of his female friends. The cops passed by, and he managed to get away. Then the woman lifted the lid of the can and said, "You need to change your life and go to the Dream Center." He took her up on the offer, climbed out of the garbage can and checked himself into the Dream Center.

The crowed at church roared in laughter at his crazy story. If ever there is a picture of rising from rock bottom, it is this. The man graduated from the program after a year. From garbage can to graduate. One small step out of a garbage can took him into a new life. During the greeting portion of the church service, I turned to my wife and said, "Rescued from a garbage can . . . I've seen it all now." It is never too late to start over.

Starting Over

The book of Acts tells us honestly about the troubled dynamics of the relationship between Paul and John Mark:

> Some time later Paul said to Barnabas, "Let us go back and visit the believers in all the towns where we preached the word of the Lord and see how they are doing." Barnabas wanted to take John, also called Mark, with them, but Paul did not think it wise to take him, because he had deserted them in Pamphylia and had not continued with them in the work. They had such a sharp disagreement that they parted company. Barnabas took Mark and sailed for Cyprus, but Paul chose Silas and left, commended by the believers to the grace of the Lord. He went through Syria and Cilicia, strengthening the churches.
>
> Acts 15:36–41

I think this is one of the most honest set of verses in the Bible. This was a feud in ministry between the apostle Paul and John Mark, the cousin of Barnabas, who had gone with Paul on a missionary journey and for some reason had departed early, leaving Paul in the lurch. To Paul, who was the kind of guy who could turn his life around radically and run tirelessly for God soon after God called him, this was unacceptable. Mark became homesick and went back to Jerusalem? Paul's do-or-die nature did not like that.

On the next missionary venture, Barnabas (whose name means "son of encouragement") tried to encourage Paul to take back John Mark as his helper. Paul basically said, "No way! That guy was a quitter. He sold me out, and I do not want that loose baggage going with me." Barnabas is that guy in the relational equation who is the bridge between two people who do not get along. We all need people like that, someone who will advocate for the future and not let us be stuck in the past.

Now, I realize that in an ideal world everyone in ministry ought to get along in perfect harmony, and there should be no divisions in the Kingdom of God. But we are all at different stages of maturity, and sometimes people need time to work through their issues. I find it fascinating that even though Paul and John Mark had conflicting priorities, God lovingly used them both anyway. Even while they were both being petty, God used them.

Sometimes we hold a grudge for too long, but God keeps patiently trying to help us bind together what was broken. In Paul's case, time moved on and apparently his wounds healed. Maybe he became more mature and began to perceive the spiritual growth in Mark, as well.

> Sometimes we hold a grudge for too long, but God keeps patiently trying to help us bind together what was broken.

Eventually the apostle summoned the man who had failed him years ago to be his friend again. Paul wrote in his letter to Timothy, "Only Luke is with me. Get Mark and bring him with you, because he is helpful to me in my ministry" (2 Timothy 4:11). Paul was in need, and who did he ask for? John Mark. Paul called him useful, even though in the past he would have said he was useless. Paul healed an old hurt by simply reaching out. He stepped out into the future. He made the decision to leave the past behind and to get back into a relationship with someone who had let him down. He later went further, by asking the people to be receptive of Mark (see Colossians 4:10). This proves that it is never too late, that God can heal, restore and re-create.

My John Mark Story

A very influential ministry made an announcement that they were coming to Los Angeles to build a new church. The church was going to be located just a few miles from ours. They approached me when they came, making their intentions known. They did all the right things, and I welcomed them into the city. Even though I did the right thing by not hindering them from coming, there was a residue of bitterness in my spirit. Never would I say a negative word about them from the pulpit, but in my heart, I had crawled up into a petty place of resentment.

Years and years passed. Finally, one day I decided to write the pastor a letter apologizing for the attitude that I had had and regretting the fact that I had not been their biggest cheerleader. It was a full-page repentance letter that expressed no self-justification and no "hear my heart on this issue."

How could I have been a barrier to the Gospel being preached? How could I have been so small-minded as to not see the bigger picture? Writing the letter was a relatively small thing, but it became a monumental building block to the future. It felt like from that point on everything in our church started to prosper. One small step back into the past cleared the roadway to the new season. Dealing with the things from the past is an important step forward toward the future.

> Dealing with the things from the past is an important step forward toward the future.

Remember:

1. It's never too late to do the right thing.
2. It's never too late for reconciliation.
3. It's never too late to start a brand-new future.
4. It's never too late to do something incredible.

The Other Side of the Miracle on Ice

I love the story of the U.S. Olympic hockey team who competed in the 1980 Olympics in Lake Placid, New York. Before the Olympics started, the Russian team had beaten the Americans in an exhibition game with a 10–3 score. They were considered unbeatable, having won four previous Olympic gold medals. The Miracle on Ice was the subsequent incredible gold medal victory that the United States won over Russia.

The Russians had first learned of hockey through the success of the Canadian hockey team. All they knew was how perfect the Canadian game was. The sport was just being introduced to the Russians, and someone said, "Why don't you just learn everything from the Canadians?"

But the Russian coach made a surprising statement. He said, "If we just copy what made the Canadians great, we will never catch up to them. We will build a future by finding our own style, so that we can go past the Canadians."

Success going forward lies in our ability to create something brand-new. The Russians, who were years behind everyone else in their mastery of the game, learned to find their own style. The coach devised some of the most bizarre workouts anyone has ever seen. He studied ballet and incorporated it into his hockey coaching. (Picture big, tough hockey players doing ballet!) He made them practice tumbling like gymnasts, for when they would need it on the ice. They did not have one great scorer, so they developed a strategy in which they all flowed together in a well-orchestrated symphony of smooth teamwork.

Yes, the United States won the gold medal at the Olympics that year, but behind that one loss was the creation of a Russian hockey superpower that would change the sport for years. They built a new identity for the future. Late to the sport, they nevertheless proved that it is never too late to re-create.

Never Too Late

It was not too late for the thief on the cross. In his last few dying minutes, he gasped out one final request—to be saved—and Jesus said yes. In his one final breath, he called upon Jesus for mercy, and he found eternal life. He dared to believe that he still had a future.

Could you dare to give God one last breath? One single word terrifies the enemy: *Start!* It is hard to get started sometimes. (Remember in high school when any distraction was enough to keep you from getting started on your homework?) Rather than regretting that your Bible is collecting dust, just open it up and get going. The Bible says, "Though the righteous fall seven times, they rise again, but the wicked stumble when calamity strikes" (Proverbs 24:16). An honest person is not afraid to start again. The wicked sink into a deeper hole because they simply do not want to start again.

Colonel Sanders, before he was selling Kentucky Fried Chicken, was selling Michelin tires and working on the railroads. He did not start marketing his famous chicken until he was 62 years old. Ever since then he has been making us all a little tighter in the belt across the country. It is never too late to start a new career. Cruise control

190

is not an option; we will always have more dreams to dream, more grudges to let go and more new attitudes to embrace.

Stan Lee didn't create Spider-Man until he was 40 years of age. Peter Roget did not publish the thesaurus until he was 75 years old. Jesus did not start His public ministry until He was 30.

> We will always have more dreams to dream, more grudges to let go and more new attitudes to embrace.

"Give me my mountain!"

How about Caleb? I always laugh when I read his story. (You can find it in Numbers 13 and 14, and more in Joshua 14.) When Caleb was 85 years of age, he declared, "I am just as strong today as I was as a boy." It had been 40 years since Caleb had voted to go into the Promised Land. He and Joshua had come back from spying on the territory with a good report: "Yes, there are giants in the land, but we can do it."

When the other spies said, "The giants are so big we look like grasshoppers," Caleb and Joshua's hopes were crushed as they were outvoted. Then, for 40 years, they had to roam the wilderness with the unbelieving generation of people who said it could not be done. They had to pay the penalty for the others' lack of faith. Even though Caleb's body roamed the wilderness, his heart was in the Promised Land all those years. (Dreams might be delayed, but if your heart is alive, you are still in position for a miracle.)

One thing I especially love about Caleb is that he did not use people's lack of faith to kill his dream. He did not say, bitterly, "We could have had it if not for all the people who messed it up." He kept his love for the future alive—and his trust in God's promises. Finally, much later in life, when he saw the Promised Land with his own eyes again, Caleb stood up and said, "Give me my mountain." Forty years of disappointment had only made him hungrier to get his promise.

Caleb got his mountain; he got his land. It took a lot longer than it should have, but it was worth the wait for old man Caleb. Life is full of ups and downs and seasons that change, but if you stay alive spiritually and keep hopeful about the future, you just might hang around long enough to reach a new launching point for what God wants you to do next.

> Life is full of ups and downs and seasons that change, but if you stay alive spiritually and keep hopeful about the future, you just might hang around long enough to reach a new launching point for what God wants you to do next.

Every time we survive a quitting moment, we position ourselves for opportunity. Stepping into the future boldly may not always look like much. By simply showing up and sticking it out during the tough times, as Caleb did for 40 years of his life in the desert, he had a real chance for a miracle.

Give yourself a chance to experience a miracle by showing up with a positive attitude about what tomorrow can be like.

Blast through the Barriers

One thing that running all those marathons taught me is that in a long-distance race there are not only physical challenges, but also different emotional barriers you must endure. Running 26.2 miles is not a walk in the park.

The first phase is the joyful phase. You line up at the starting line full of energy. The crowd atmosphere is electric, music is pumping and you feel alive. By the time you have run the first ten miles, you start to feel your first tinges of discomfort. Your body gently reminds you that it feels something, but it is not bad enough to make you stop.

The famous wall arrives somewhere between miles eighteen and twenty, and that is when every part of your body throbs with pain. The glycogen stored up in your body has run out. It is then that you have to decide if the pain is worth reaching the finish line and if the reward is worth the sacrifice. If you can just keep going long enough to reach the final mile, hope will keep you alive, and you will cross the line with no regrets.

There are definitely moments in your life where you must hang on to your dream and slug it out until courage returns. I am sure that Caleb had moments when he almost gave up. But he always turned back toward the Promised Land. He decided to hang on. His dream was delayed, but 40 years later it was fulfilled.

Running on Hope

The Dream Center has had many memorable moments. I will never forget the day we bought the hospital. My father, who was 60 years old at the time, ran all the way from Phoenix to Los Angeles to kick off the fundraising campaign to raise money for the Dream Center. (Yes, crazy runs are in our blood. He ran four hundred miles through the desert to raise support for the Dream Center.)

The final stretch of the run took my father down Hollywood Boulevard toward the Queen of Angels Hospital, which is now the Dream

Center. Hundreds of us met him there, and we ran the final stretch of seven miles with him. Together, we raised enough money to get into the building and to get started.

There were times when we have needed thousands of dollars on short notice, and God has always showed up. Some days I ask God if I can get off the roller coaster of survival for one week and just cruise on Easy Street, but He has always kept giving us just enough provision to survive—but more than enough hope for the future. I think I would rather have more hope for the future and struggle for survival than for things to come easily and to start to feel entitled to the blessings.

I would rather have more hope for the future and struggle for survival than for things to come easily and to start to feel entitled to the blessings.

There are certainly some dreams that have not been fulfilled, but like Caleb, I am going to keep talking about taking over that mountain because if I let go of my faith for the future, I will start to die on the inside.

How about you? I urge you to keep moving forward toward your future. You might move an inch or a mile at a time. You might have to survive the winds of adversity pushing you back. But if you respond to every challenge with some type of forward-moving response, you will get there.

I have learned that when we consider adversity to be a meaningless, unnecessary intrusion into our lives, we lose the power to be a giant for God. In order to continue to be a Caleb, you have got to be tested; that is how you will be able to maintain your fighter's edge. Somehow in the last decade or so, it has become fashionable in the Church to believe that as a privileged child of God, you will avoid the storms of life and the obligation to prepare for them. Have you fallen for that idea?

The Eye of the Tiger

A phrase that came out of the Vietnam War is "the eye of the tiger." It refers to a combat veteran who was wounded in battle but who comes back to fight. He gets hit by the enemy, but comes back with a vengeance that is unending, unstoppable and awe-inspiring. The fierceness of soldiers once wounded who recover is phenomenal. They keep stepping up and moving forward even when the battle rages hotly. The smoke will clear, and that soldier will be the one standing.

Life can steal your opportunities; it can stack the cards against you; it can even seem to war against you. However, it cannot take away your eye of the tiger, which makes you resilient in setbacks.

You can decide to have a good attitude whenever you want to, you know. The Bible has a lot to say about choices. Before crossing into the Promised Land, Joshua was surrounded by a generation of people who did not believe in God's promise. Joshua made a bold statement about turning one's will to embrace the future:

> But if serving the Lord seems undesirable to you, then choose for your-selves this day whom you will serve, whether the gods your ancestors served beyond the Euphrates, or the gods of the Amorites, in whose land you are living. But as for me and my household, we will serve the Lord.
>
> Joshua 24:15

Joshua made a choice. He chose to live with the frame of mind of possibility and faith. All of life is a choice, everything in it. We may think circumstances determine what will happen during the day, but no, the choices we make determine everything. Joshua narrowed the moment down to a choice: Are we going forward or are we going backward? Choose. His speech was simple and direct, and the people were forced to make up their minds. Living in the middle was not an option. The days of drifting through the wilderness were over, and it was time to embrace a new life, making bold decisions.

No More Pity Parties

Live your life as an attack-oriented thinker. Do not wait for good things to happen first to determine if you will respond the right way. With God's help, you can take the worst of circumstances and find joy and purpose even in those moments.

I remember one day I was having a personal pity party and inwardly complaining about my lot in life. I was flying back from speaking at a church, and for some reason I allowed a melancholy spirit to take hold of my heart. I was pacing up and down the lobby of the airport, bothered by insignificant things.

> Do not wait for good things to happen first to determine if you will respond the right way. With God's help, you can take the worst of circumstances and find joy and purpose even in those moments.

Then out of the corner of my eye I saw a very touching scene. A father was with his boy who was in a wheelchair, carefully attending to his needs. I have seen so many loving parents with their children in wheelchairs, but this was an especially moving sight. The dad was wiping the food off his little boy's face with so much love. It is hard for me to explain, but it looked like

196

every single wipe had the love of Jesus all over it. The boy would make loud noises, and the father would lovingly calm him down and gently stroke his hand.

The level of patience expressed by this father was positively angelic. At one point, he lifted the boy's body to put him into a more comfortable position in his chair, and every act of service was done with such delicate ease. Nothing appeared to be an unwelcome obligation; all of it was done with the utmost attention to detail. I did not see one ounce of frustration in this father who had to deal with a crippled boy in an inconvenient place. He did everything with the expression of a man who was proud of his son.

It humbled me, and seeing them together delivered me from a meaningless pity party that I should have canceled before it started. If that man could have so much love and hope for his son in a wheelchair, what is stopping me from having hope for tomorrow?

Honor and Serve

One day I got a phone call from a pastor friend of mine who told me that Oral Roberts was turning 90 years of age, and my friend was looking to see if we were interested in having him at our church for a birthday celebration. Oral was not seeking this but my friend was. Honestly, I was shocked that he was even looking for a church to host this giant of the faith. I found out that a few churches that were closer to his home in Orange County turned down the request due to their uncompromising schedule. I learned a long time ago to never be a slave to a church schedule, but rather to be flexible and ready to change in a moment's time. I also feel badly that just because people are older, we tend to think that their best years are over and fail to make a priority of honoring them.

I said, "Sure, we would love to have Dr. Roberts." They drove him from Orange County to our midweek service in Los Angeles. I had never met Oral Roberts, and now I was hosting his ninetieth birthday party! We introduced him and invited him to say a few words. I was amazed at how much faith he had to believe for the future. He was 90 years old, but he was not talking much at all about the past.

He said things like, "Expect a miracle!" and every single word that came out of his mouth had to do with great expectations. I thought that most of what he was going to say would be flashback stories of his healing crusades or other events. I would have understood if he had done that, but instead his focus was on tomorrow. He was in the final years of his life, but there was a twinkle of tomorrow in his eyes. It was then that I realized age is just a number, and being forever young means boldly declaring a brighter future.

The crowd cheered with every word that he spoke, and it was a glorious night. It is interesting that Dr. Roberts' healing crusades ministered to broken people. Now at the end of his life, his ministry came full circle to a different type of broken people who need Jesus.

As the service was coming to an end, the Lord told me to receive an offering for him, for the future of Dr. Roberts' ministry. The pastor that had arranged the celebration had not wanted us to give him a penny; he just wanted Oral to be loved on. I wrestled with God about that for a moment. I thought, *God, I am going to sound crazy receiving an offering for a man at the very, very end of his life. He is not preaching anymore. Why should I receive a ministry offering for him?*

Obedience prevailed, and I decided to do it anyway, specifically for the future of Oral Roberts. The offering was counted, and it was $72,000. One man gave a $50,000 check in that offering. I called my pastor friend and told him I wanted to bring the check over and hand deliver it to Dr. Roberts. Have you ever had such a wonderful gift to give someone that you could not sleep the night before? This is exactly how I felt. That check was burning a hole in my pocket. I promised my friend that I would show up, give Dr. Roberts the check and get out of there in under a minute, as I did not want to disrespect this giant of the faith by lingering at his house.

My assistant and I pulled up to his humble little condo. We walked in, and it was not what I was expecting. It was just a tiny place in a very ordinary location. I had been under the misconception that this man who spoke of so much faith and victory would live in a mansion. But the truth was that he had given much of what he had away.

He greeted us graciously, and my goal was to give him the check and get out of there as quickly as possible, but he would have none of that. He opened the check and saw that gigantic number and was visibly overwhelmed by what this inner-city church had done for him. He grabbed my hand, prayed for blessing upon our church and then proceeded to pour into my life for an hour. He mentored me with every ounce of love a man could possess.

You would expect someone like that to mentor you by telling you what you need to do, speaking directly and boldly into your life. This has not been my experience. Every legendary leader I have spent time with has just loved on me. Completely taken aback by this experience, I expressed my gratitude for being allowed to bring the check over, and my friend later told me that all day long Dr. Roberts would just sit and talk to pastors, pouring out his love and wisdom and anointing into them. He was using the final years of his life to minister to leaders one-on-one.

> Every legendary leader I have spent time with has just loved on me.

Then I realized why God had told me to receive an offering for the future of his ministry. This man was still giving and serving, willing to be poured out all the way to the end. The future was still on his mind, and he was addicted to serving. He understood that if you have a pulse, you have a purpose. His life was well lived and still moving forward. To this day, many pastors talk about the legendary final moments of Dr. Roberts's life and how something he told them turned the tide in their ministry. He was fighting for the heart and soul of each one of them until the end.

My prayer is that no matter what you are going through, when you read this simple story, you will understand that your best days are not behind you. They are the ones—today, for instance!—when you choose to live in hope for the future.

MY SMALL STEP 12

After reading about this step and taking some time to pray, write down the small step you will take to follow God's nudge.

STEP 13

Leave a Local Legacy

I love the term *hometown heroes*. It always makes me feel warm on the inside. The idea that someone can be a local janitor at a school for years, and generations of kids adore him or her as a hometown hero, clearly proves how anyone can leave a mark in life. When a local coach stays at the same high school for decades, he puts his stamp of consistency upon an entire community. Hometown heroes are inspiring.

I routinely go to the donut shop down the street, where I read the local newspaper, *La Crescenta*. It is a tiny publication; I find it refreshing to read local news without the daily trashing of people that we see in the national news. Every hometown paper in America should highlight the good character traits and even godly virtues of the citizens in their community, because it helps to pass on those traits to others.

One day while I was reading the local paper, I started thinking, *How can God's people leave a clear and noticeable mark on the world?* Then I realized that the best way to change the world is for God's people to do a lot of small things with great faithfulness.

The Dream Center is a big building, but the things we are best known for have nothing to do with the big building and everything to do with little acts of kindness that never stop happening. Consistency is the secret to the Dream Center. We have been showing up and having children's church programs in the inner city for over twenty years in some neighborhoods. The other day I was at a shopping center, and a man in his thirties came up to me and said, "Pastor Barnett, I need to talk to you." At first I was scared, because he had such a serious look on his face. (Maybe it was my guilty conscience, but I thought he was going to give it to me.)

> The best way to change the world is for God's people to do a lot of small things with great faithfulness.

A tear rolled down his face as he talked about being a boy who was raised in the projects and how nothing in his life was ever consistent. He never had one person who showed up for him and fulfilled promises. He said the only consistent, positive thing he had in his life was the Dream Center truck showing up every week. This was an old ice cream truck converted into a mobile children's church vehicle, and it was the only thing that did not let him down. He shook my hand and said, "Thanks for never leaving the 'hood," and he walked off.

The most important thing we can do to impact our culture is to simply show up for people. Mother Teresa led an incredible outreach to help the masses of the poor in India and other countries. When someone asked her, "What is the secret to changing the world?" her answer was shockingly simple. She said, "If you want to change the world, go home and love your family." Such a wonderful, simple answer!

She understood one thing about legacy: No matter how you define legacy, it is built by just being available for people. It is not the size and scope of anything; it is the simplicity of showing up with consistency.

It starts at home. I remember the many times my dad would cancel preaching trips just to be home for one of my games. In spite of the fact that my dad was one of the most in-demand speaker-pastors in America at the time, I would see him at every important practice and every game. He never missed one important thing in my life. I think that is one of the reasons I keep showing up for my own family and community—because my dad showed up for me. Thus the attribute of consistency gets passed down from one generation to the next, and legacies are passed on through ordinary acts of kindness.

> The most important thing we can do to impact our culture is to simply show up for people.

Leaving a local legacy means that you start living the way you want to remembered. Your legacy can be an attribute of character or the way you handle suffering. We all have something unique to pass on to others, and what we are passionate about is what we will leave behind.

Much of what we will leave as a legacy is hard to define, but sometimes a character trait such as self-sacrifice or bravery defines a moment in time and a person becomes what we call a hero. I am always amazed how, in the midst of the horror of a school shooting, some student or staff member always comes forward as a hero, stepping in front of the shooter to take a bullet for someone else. It seems that with every story of tragedy, there is also a story of self-sacrifice. In some cases, one act of courage can leave a local or even national legacy of self-sacrifice.

It is true that we may waste years of our lives with meaningless living, only to rise to an occasion and do something heroic and life-changing. It is never too late to be a servant and never too late to do one meaningful act. My favorite movies are always the ones where villains reach out and do one final good deed before they die. The act does not right all of the wrongs they have done, but it does show that redemptive acts can come out of wasted years.

God has a way of turning hometown villains into hometown heroes. Most of my core staff at the Dream Center is made up of people who wasted most of their earlier years living in darkness. By darkness, I do not mean people who stole a piece of candy at a store or even cheated on their spouse in former years. I mean people who slammed a needle into their veins in dark alleys and spent years of their lives looking for someone to mug to support their habit, or men who shot up rival gangs, the kind of people who would be considered villains in any movie script. I see them now scattered all over the Dream Center campus, running the kitchen, giving away free meals, working in our clothing store, giving away garments to the homeless. They are preaching the Gospel and a few are even pastoring churches. They represent the revolutionary transformation of a local agent of terror to a local hero. Their lives prove that even if we spend a good part of our years doing evil, the few years that we have to do good will prevail.

> It is never too late to be a servant and never too late to do one meaningful act.

Jacob Hurley

The man who runs the Dream Center food truck, Jacob Hurley, is an uncommon local hero. For years, Jacob roamed the streets of Los Angeles robbing, stealing and running with gangs; he had become a menace to the community. The rescue missions would not even take him in because he was too far gone.

Just one look at Jacob could tell you that this was a man who was out to do something destructive. He was slamming drugs at such a rate that his life was on the line every day. One day a rescue mission told him to go to the Dream Center. He arrived in the middle of the night and asked to use the restroom, and then he went wandering through the halls of the Dream Center. A man working security, who had graduated from the rehab program, told him about the program. In a rare moment of vulnerability, Jacob decided to give it a try. He was not committed to the idea but was at least willing to do something to get off the street.

From that day forward, Jacob's life was transformed, one small act of kindness at a time. His every act of hostility was greeted by unconditional love, and the walls he had built for years and years all came down.

Some people will test the limits of our love to see if it is real, and Jacob was one of them. But when we keep showing them kindness, they run out of excuses to behave a certain way and the love of Christ always wins. When people lash out at you, consider it a compliment. You might be the only person they are testing because they see you as the last standard of goodness left to challenge. Jacob kept looking for reasons to run, but he could not find any. He was swept away in the current of the other men's kindness. The Dream Center campus just swallowed him up with love, vision, purpose and a new identity.

People like Jacob are looking for every possible way to fail and to excuse themselves from believing something good can happen to them. Give them no reason to believe that. Local heroes full of God's grace will not give up on destructive people, and they will not let the past win. When people try to walk over them, heroes in God's

Kingdom do not see it as being used but rather as being a bridge of hope—which is meant to be walked on—linking people from their past to their future. These heroes in God's Kingdom are spending their lives advocating for people like Jacob. They see no reason to hide from broken people, because they know that the love they have is always greater than the pain the broken people carry. Instead of spending their lives protesting behavior they do not like, they confront destructive behavior with consistent, relentless love.

The world is relentless in doing wrong. Let's become relentless in doing what is right!

Jacob graduated from our recovery program, which seemed like a major chapter in his life at the time, but now it seems rather small compared to what he has become. Today Jacob runs our mobile food trucks that go to 41 locations a week. Think about the magnitude of that for just a second. At every site they visit, they give away two hundred grocery bags filled with food to needy families. Multiply two hundred bags by 41 sites and you can see that he is feeding many thousands of people a week, literally the population of a decent-sized city.

In addition to that ministry, Jacob has what I call the ministry of inconvenience. He will stop everything at the drop of a hat to help anyone on campus with their ministry, even though he runs one of the largest ministries at the Dream Center. There is no other way to put it—he has become addicted to serving. He's a junky for Jesus, a man who loves to overdose on doing good.

When Jacob goes out on the food truck, some of the moms he feeds are some of the same moms he used to rob. At first, they looked at him the same way people looked at the apostle Paul after his conversion, highly skeptical that Paul could change that much. Jacob's story parallels Paul's, because he has the community scratching their collective heads trying to figure out how one man's life can be so different from what it was before. I love it when God transforms a broken life so much that eventually you forget that person was ever a criminal.

There are many heroes in this story. The night security man who told him about the program; the people who loved him in the program; the head of all the ministry programs at the Dream Center, the woman who told me she thought he was the man to run the food truck when there was a job opening. (I thought she was crazy, but she saw something I could not see.)

Even in smaller communities, there is a town drunk or a wild kid in high school that everyone has given up on. But by God's grace, there are also people who will stand up to them with an intense love that extends beyond their bad choices. The world we live in is all about seek and destroy, overpower through force, get what you want and tear down reputations to get ahead. But there will always be those who are agents of change, people who lift the burdens of others and who are keeping communities strong through simple service and a heart that never stops advocating for change.

Leaving a legacy also means modeling godly traits for others. My father-in-law, Clarence, has done that. I have been married to his daughter for over two decades, and I have never, ever seen him angry, not even one time. His kindness is so consistent that everyone marvels at it. Clarence grew up in Sweden. He immigrated to the United States and started various businesses, going through many hard times because of the cultural barriers and a few bad business start-ups. Struggling to find a place for his family, his spirit sustained him through many dark times.

Clarence is a prime example of how one great perfected attribute can leave a legacy. His one great survival tactic for life is to crank up joy when life brings sorrow. He is now the director of the prison ministry at the Dream Center. He has so much respect within the notorious

Men's Central Jail in downtown Los Angeles that they allow him to minister to prisoners who are in solitary confinement. The prisoners who test him simply cannot win. He is a man you cannot offend. His love for people is so strong that you might as well just give up trying to confront him. He is not street-smart, and he cannot relate to many of the guys in the prison in terms of street credibility. The one thing he does have is kindness credibility, and it works.

I think a great misconception about reaching people is to assume that you must be able to relate to their lives in order to reach them. It helps, but it is not necessary. Prisoners can yell at him, throw urine at him, call him names and test every ounce of his patience, but they will not win. His heart has been touched by God's love and that love can outlast anything. Eventually they will listen to what he says because he has earned the right to be heard.

I am always seeing people who are living at the Dream Center that Clarence visited in prison. His life reminds me of this Scripture: "Everyone has heard about your obedience, so I rejoice because of you; but I want you to be wise about what is good, and innocent about what is evil. The God of peace will soon crush Satan under your feet" (Romans 16:19–20). Take special note of the words, "everyone has heard about your obedience." It is incredible to think that something as simple as being obedient makes a far greater impact than we could ever anticipate. The other promise is that if we continue to be excellent regarding doing good, it will ultimately crush the adversary.

Clarence has made such an impact on the church that when people are in the hospital, they do not ask for me to come and visit them— they ask for Clarence. His kindness and love have become legendary, and his love carries the weight of credibility.

Each superhero has a different power. The Incredible Hulk has strength, Superman has invincibility, Batman has cool gadgets. They use their skills to fight back evil. What is your great quality? Look deep into your soul and let that power shine. Set a legacy in motion by specializing in something that reflects Jesus. It is never too late to be a superhero—or "just" a hometown hero. Even you. You may not leave a mark on society with some big thing, but the attributes you set in motion will leave a legacy for others.

> Set a legacy in motion by specializing in something that reflects Jesus.

Whispers of the King

David handpicked 37 men out of all the troops that served him, and he called them his mighty men (see 2 Samuel 23:8–38). One of them slew two top-ranked enemy warriors, killed a lion in a snowy pit and killed an Egyptian with his own spear. Another slew eight hundred soldiers at one time, single-handedly. Yet another fought so hard and long that his hand had to be pried off his sword afterward.

In other words, these men were all about fighting to the death. But what else did the three mightiest out of the mighty do? One day King David was standing in his stronghold overlooking the city of Bethlehem. In the Valley of Rephaim was a Philistine encampment; on the other side of the Philistine army was the well of Bethlehem where David used to drink as a boy. David looked over at that well and became nostalgic, talking to himself: "Someday, I would just like to drink one more time from that well." The soldiers overheard David, and one said to the other two, "Did you hear what he just said? He said, he would like to have a drink from the well of Bethlehem."

Now, David did not need to drink from that particular well. He had water already. But when these men heard the whisper of the king, they risked their lives and broke through the Philistine army in order to get David a drink of water from the Bethlehem well he used to drink from as a boy. This exploit was nowhere near as spectacular as their military victories, but in a very real way, what they did is even more amazing. They listened to the whisper of the king. They listened to his heartbeat and were quick to respond. David was humbled by this expression of attentiveness and loyalty, and it is remembered as the mightiest act of all.

These men followed the nudge of the king. They listened to the whisper of his royal heart. God may be whispering something to you, something that seems very small in comparison to a glorious public exploit. And yet your obedience could bring you heavenly acclaim, even if the people around you think that what you are doing is insignificant or even foolish. Every day in the daily routines of your life, God is whispering things for you to do. Do not ignore His voice, just because His requests seem so small. To Him, your loving response is monumental. Someone who is in tune with God will be responsive to His little nudges. God is so pleased when we do little things with a big heart. They might not ever get noticed on earth, but in heaven they are being celebrated as legacy moments, because any one of them can cause a major shift on earth.

Breaking the Stalemate

I know a man whose marriage was in a stalemate for over a decade. Both he and his wife felt hurt over past disagreements, and they both stood their ground. Neither would apologize first. They were both equally wrong, but they would not budge, in defiance over who had committed the biggest offense. Each of them fortified their tragic position of being right.

One day God spoke to this man in prayer and told him, "Can you imagine how wonderful your life could be if you took the first step?" The man thought about the big scheme of things. He thought about his children who had not seen their parents embrace in years, and he considered what it might feel like for his children to see their parents in such a loveless marriage. He thought about all the times in the past year he had driven home but did not want to walk into the house because of the chilly atmosphere. He thought about the long-dead dream of believing they could love each other again. He considered how their lives had changed for the worse simply because of a prideful relational stalemate. He let his mind drift to the future and thought further about growing old and the kind of legacy that he would leave behind: one of bitterness and petty squabbles.

He decided to take a step that he did not want to take. His pride wanted to win, but the legacy of their family was at stake along with everyone's well-being. Pride put up one final fight, but the man took a step toward repentance. He went home and bared his soul and took full responsibility for what had happened. From that moment on, everything changed. Theirs has become a model marriage. One step of humility was all it took.

How much could your life change if you decided to go ahead and do that hard thing you have been holding back from doing? Why not just give the other person what you have been withholding from them, basing your decision on the fact that making peace is more important than being the winner? Take a step toward defeating arrogance and reversing the greatest weaknesses of your life by simply deciding in your heart to refuse to settle for anything less than God's very best. Your life can be better. A new legacy is born whenever you move to defeat your greatest weaknesses, which are like your biggest giants.

Remember David and Goliath (see 1 Samuel 17). The gigantic Philistine came out every morning and night to taunt the people of God. He would step up, and the people would stand down. Same thing every day, same fears, same result. David finally stepped up to take on the giant, and he flattened him. As soon as he defeated the giant, a new surge of faith arose in the people, and they rushed onto the battlefield, suddenly full of courage. Here is the point! It takes only one person to start a new pattern and new legacy. Everyone's confidence came from David's one act of faith.

The world is waiting for us to set aside our hesitation, establish a pattern of good works and leave a legacy of compassion in our daily world. Each one of us has distinct weaknesses, and we must usually grapple with at least one major issue of life before we can break free. It is the barrier to leaving a legacy. David understood that he did not have to be a great warrior to defeat Goliath; he simply had to be a person who would show up and make himself available for God's use. It can be the same for us as we let our greatest strengths shine and confront our greatest weaknesses head on in the battlefield.

Take Those Baby Steps

The greatest joy in my life is going to the Dream Center and seeing all the tired, homeless people checking in for the program. Some are so strung out they appear to be on the edge of death. The reason I love to see them in that condition is not because I like to see people in pain; I want to get a mental snapshot of who they are now versus who they will become. I know they will be healthy again, and I know they will dream again. I know that their families will start to come together. I know that eventually they will look nothing like their picture on the intake badge.

I know all of this because I know the reputation of my God, and I know what He is able to do. Their hands may be shaking because of alcohol withdrawal as they fill out the application, but it will not always be that way. Tears of sorrow will turn into tears of joy. The day will come when they will clap, sing and rejoice. The generations after them will be forever changed. They have taken a courageous step, and they do not even know how courageous it is.

God is so pleased when we take a small step of faith; it is what He has been waiting for. He awaits your next courageous step. A single act of faith can change everything. Just as when a small child learns to walk and his parent is right there to catch him if he falls, so God is waiting for you to take those baby steps, and He rejoices in being the One who helps you when you fall.

In the movie *What about Bob?* my favorite scene is when the challenging patient Bob, who lives in constant fear, has an appointment with the egotistical Dr. Leo Marvin. The doctor gives Bob his book, titled *Baby Steps*. Marvin explains that the book is about setting goals for yourself that are reasonable and then taking baby steps toward achieving them. Marvin explains to Bob, "When you leave this office, do not think about everything you have to do to get out of the building. Just deal with getting out of the room. When you reach the hall, just deal with the hall. And so forth. Baby steps." Bob is captivated by the concept. The revelation goes off like a rocket in his soul. He gets up and starts to take baby steps around the room. He opens the door and tells the psychiatrist, "It works. It works! All I have to do is take one little step at a time, and I can do anything."

It is a funny scene, but it is true, especially when you are walking in the footsteps of a God who loves you and goes before you. As long as you keep taking a few steps forward, anything becomes possible. "Do not despise these small beginnings, for the Lord rejoices to see the

> As long as you keep taking a few steps forward, anything becomes possible.

work begin" (Zechariah 4:10 NLT). God is pleased when you take baby steps of faith, and He is eager to see your legacy of faith as it develops. Move those feet forward and walk with Him. Walk together with Him on your journey and never look back!

MY SMALL STEP 13

After reading about this step and taking some time to pray, write down the small step you will take to follow God's nudge.

Matthew Barnett is senior pastor of the historic Angelus Temple and the Dream Center in Los Angeles, California, now one of over 150 Dream Centers around the world. He and his father, megachurch pastor Tommy Barnett, co-founded the L.A. Dream Center under the auspices of the Assemblies of God in 1994. In 2001, the Dream Center was formally united with Angelus Temple, the flagship Foursquare church founded by Aimee Semple McPherson. A congregation of over 7,000 now attends weekly, and the Dream Center reaches more than 30,000 people weekly with its needs-based ministries and outreaches.

Matthew is in demand across the country as a speaker for churches, conferences and camp meetings, and, with George Barna, is the author of the bestselling book *The Cause within You*. His other books include *The Church That Never Sleeps* and *Misfits Welcome*.

Matthew and his wife, Caroline, have a daughter and a son, and they make their home in the Los Angeles area.

—Visit—
matthewbarnett.com
dreamcenter.org
thedcnetwork.org
angelustemple.org